How To Lead
A Winning Group

How To Lead
A Winning Group

David Barber

Insight Network Marketing Library

 SIGHT

How To Lead A Winning Group
David Barber

Insight Publishing Ltd
Sterling House
Church Street
Ross-on-Wye
Herefordshire
HR9 5HN

Phone: 01989-564496
Fax: 01989-565596

Notice of Liability

While great care has been taken in the preparation of this publication, it should not be used as a substitute for appropriate professional advice. Neither the author nor Insight Publishing can accept any liability for loss or damage occasioned by any person acting as a result of the material in this book.

Acknowledgement

The Business Activity Agreement (BACTA) has been developed from an idea originally discussed with Martin Kern. Many distributors have use the idea with great success, and I, and they, are greatly indebted to Martin.

ISBN: 1-899298-05-3

Cover design by Just Proportion, Louth, Lincolnshire
Cartoons by James Hutcheson Design, Edinburgh
Printed in Finland by WSOY

I dedicate this book and the whole
of the S.T.A.R. Leadership Programme
to those distributors with
the drive to solve their ATAC Equation,
the wisdom to learn,
the determination to act,
and who care enough about their people's success
to want to show them the way.

Contents

Introduction

Anyone Can Be A Winning Teacher And Leader

One of the most exciting things in life is to watch people, under your care and guidance and through a series of simple steps, create sometimes awesome outcomes. That is what winning *teachers* do. One of the most exciting gifts you can give anyone is the opportunity to make something of their own lives: to give them the vehicle, by your inspiration show them how to use it and then take them to heights of which they had previously only dreamt. That is what winning *leaders* do.

The day you recruit your first distributor is the day you become a group leader. With that, goes the responsibility for showing them the way. This involves the two distinct skills I have just mentioned: leadership and teaching.

Many people want to be leaders. One reason why few succeed is because, although the desire is there, they do not know *how* to and there is no-one to show them. *If you worry that you do not have the makings of leadership within you, or that you have no previous experience of teaching or leadership— don't!* I have written this book *specifically* for the vast majority who are *not* natural leaders, to take you from where you are now to wherever you want to go—the very top of the tree, if you wish.

I have therefore pitched this book at those of you who have no knowledge of teaching and leadership, indeed no experience of any form of business or executive jobs. It is the success of those of you with no such advantages that gives me by far the greatest pleasure.

So I make no apology if much what I say is obvious to others of you. Just remember that it will not be so to many of your people and, for you, the purpose of this book and the S.T.A.R. Leadership Programme is to help you in your mission to turn as many of your people as possible into successful leaders and teachers. For therein lies your own prosperity.

The S.T.A.R. Leadership Programme

This book is the climax of the S.T.A.R. Leadership Programme, the first complete home-learning and tuition programme in the industry. S.T.A.R. stands for The Four Must-Do Activities:

Sponsor

Teach

Attitudes

Retail.

The previous titles in the Programme are:

• *Get Off To A Winning Start In Network Marketing*

• *Breakthrough Sponsoring & Retailing*

The Programme also has two complimentary titles. A good knowledge of the fascinating field of **Personal Development** is an essential part of being a winning teacher and leader. This is covered in *Network Marketeers... Supercharge Yourself!*

In addition, success comes, not from action, but from *focused* or *directed* action. This means that *planning* for success is also an essential skill for you to both practise and teach. The easy way to get your people into this habit with the minimum of work from you is to introduce them to my book *Target Success!* This valuable aid includes all the forms your distributors will need for planning during the whole of their first year (including everything they need for their Contact List), and it also offers an easy way to deal with uninspiring but essential topics such as how to do their accounts.

We have already covered all the basic knowledge, techniques and attitudes which you need to pass on to your people in the earlier titles of the S.T.A.R. Leadership Programme; the purpose of this book is to show you how to pass on that information in the best possible way. It is *not* to teach you that information.

So, just as there is not a lot of point in getting into a racing car until you have learnt how to drive, if you have not familiarised yourself with the other titles in the S.T.A.R. Leadership Programme, can I suggest that you do so before going any further, otherwise much of what follows will not be clear to you. This book is concerned only with:

• How to be a winning teacher

• How to be a winning leader.

Before we cover these topics in more detail in Parts II and III, Part I will give you a general understanding of what teaching and leading mean in network marketing.

A number of terms were introduced earlier in the Programme. These are covered in a Glossary at the back of this book.

Feed yourself in bite-size chunks!

There is a great deal of valuable detail in this book. Don't blow yourself out of the Programme by forcing yourself too fast!

I would much rather that you spend a week on each chapter and apply it properly, rather than rush through it and overwhelm yourself. In the first case, you will become a winning teacher and leader; in the second, you will not.

~ ~ ~

'Give me your determination, give me your action, give me your willingness to learn, and I will show you the way'

That is my commitment to you. By the end of this Programme, you will be able to make the same commitment to your people. No matter how little natural ability, management or business experience you have, at the completion of our journey together, you, too, will have all the knowledge you need to become a winning leader and teacher, whether your aim is to build a small but profitable group, or to join those elite few who have reached the dizzy heights at the top of a profession where incomes are measured in six figures a *month*.

Part I

Teaching And Leadership: What Do They Mean In Network Marketing?

Because we are talking about teachers and leaders, there is a danger that people will read this as suggesting that teachers and leaders are different to distributors. They are not.

Where teaching is concerned, ALL distributors are teachers

Teaching is one of the Four Must-Do Activities. Through the principle of **Working With,** *a maxim of the S.T.A.R. Leadership Programme is that teaching the job* **is** *doing it, and doing the job* **is** *teaching it.*

Therefore, every distributor is a teacher and every teacher is a distributor. So when we talk about teachers, we mean one aspect of a distributor's job, which is teaching.

All distributors also become leaders to some extent, but it is your choice whether you choose a high-level or low-level role. Therefore, when we talk about leaders, we are still talking about distributors carrying out an aspect of a distributor's role.

Chapter 1

Do I Have What It Takes To Be A Leader And Teacher?

Before we discuss whether you have what it takes to be a leader and teacher, let's answer this question:

'Do I *have* to be a leader and teacher?'

With regard to being a leader, the answer is: Yes! Everyone who sponsors someone else immediately becomes a leader, whether they like it or not, with the responsibility to guide their people.

But there is no need to panic: you won't need to become another Winston Churchill! If your only aim is to build a small or medium-sized group and you do not want to become an active leader, remember the **Figure-of-Eight Attitude** (Chapter 7, *Get Off To A Winning Start*):

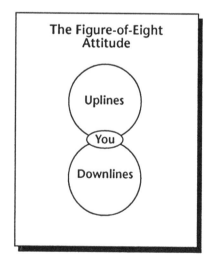

As the link between your people and your uplines, you can plug your group into the uplines who have taken on the active leadership role of the group to which you belong. That will make you a good leader. So you do not have to be an *active* leader provided that you link your people in to someone who is.

However, you must still give your people a good example by encouraging them to Stay On-Track, to take the right actions, to go to meetings and trainings, and by supporting your uplines' efforts to create a strong, successful group. Finally, you must still be prepared to help your downline distributors to overcome doubts and problems.

With regard to being a teacher, you do not need to become a public speaker but you must Work With your people as much as you can, otherwise you are not discharging your responsibility to show them what they need to do. I will explain later what Working With will involve.

There is only one exception to this. If you are one of the very rare breed of charismatic leaders (see page 29), it is a waste of your talents for the group not to make as much use of that as you can. It may be better for everyone if you arrange with your people that you will concentrate on the high profile roles (these will become obvious later) and leave them free to devote their time to teaching the group.

'What talent do I need?'

Let's get two things into perspective:

First, success as a leader and teacher only means knowing what to say when, and knowing what to do when, with the right attitudes. So, like anything else in network marketing,

> **It is not what you've got that matters, it is what you learn, what you do and how you do it**

Second:

Being a winning teacher or leader does *not* mean having to be better at the job than anyone else!

Many people think they are not good enough at the job to teach or lead. There is a lot in common between being a good network marketing teacher and a good sports coach; Coach Charles is a top sports coach and we will be talking to him later. He isn't very good at his sport, yet he is reckoned to be one of the best people around at helping other people to excel in that field. In fact, almost *no* coach in the world is as good at their sport as their top athletes. Many are not even as good at the sport as their *worst!* If you think about it, the job of a sports coach is to show people how to do the job better than the coach can—in fact, *vastly* better than they can.

Your job as a winning teacher is not to do the job well yourself, it is to help other people to be as good as *they* can, or want to, be.

Your job as a winning teacher is to be the best you can be at *teaching* it, not at *doing* it

---

In any other business I would say that if you want to be best at doing a job, then do it, don't teach it! But network marketing is peculiar in that both teaching the job and doing it are integral: as I said before, doing the job *is* teaching it and teaching the job *is* doing it.

Being no great shakes at retailing and sponsoring is no barrier to becoming a very big business-builder, if you take leadership and teaching seriously. I have been privileged to sit in on Get-Active phone calls and Two-to-Ones with some of the great business-builders. Some, yes, were real artists on the phone and at sponsoring and retailing. But many others really are no better than 'OK', yet they have big businesses. You see, they understand the Keystone Law (see page 24). They know that getting the best out of other people is much more important than how good or bad they themselves happen to be at sponsoring and retailing. In fact,

---

Being good at a job can actually be a disadvantage! Some of the best sponsors and retailers make the worst leaders and teachers

---

...unless they learn to delegate. If you know you do not do a job well, you will make it your business to teach other people to do it as well as they can to make up for your shortcomings. But a person who knows that they are good very often spends too much time doing the job instead of carrying out their function as a winning leader, which is to help *other people* to be good at it. Many leaders who insist on taking over a job (and how infuriating they are!), instead of letting their people get on with it, do so out of a belief that their people cannot do it as well as they can.

Being good at a job can also lead to impatience with others who are not as good at it as you are. You need to guard against demotivating people by thinking, *Why can't they do it properly? It seems so simple to me!* You need to hold back from the temptation to push people along at a speed which is too fast for them (in other words, play *CUPID—Unfold at their speed*—see Glossary), because the final result could be that you make them worse than they were before. You may even increase their chances of dropping out by undermining their belief that they can learn to do the job adequately.

I said it in both previous titles of the Programme but it bears repeating: there is nothing difficult about teaching or leading. The whole nub of both is that, if you trust someone *enough*, like them *enough* and respect them *enough*, you will learn anything from them and trust them as a leader. Therefore, the more people trust, like and respect you, the more willing they will be to learn from you and follow you. These are all qualities which make a wonderful human being and which anyone can develop. You will see nothing there about having to be good at your job, articulate, attractive, intelligent or well-educated. Although all these will help if you are trusted, liked and respected, *none of them will make up for a lack of those qualities.*

Anyone who can respond to a mission can be a leader

Do you doubt that, if your own child was lost and there were no emergency services available to mount a search, you could mobilise friends, neighbours and passers-by into action? If you can be a leader under those circumstances, you can be a leader under *any* circumstances. You just need to feel strongly enough about your success.

I apologise to dustmen and farm labourers when I ask this question, but would you class them as natural leaders? Yet, when Christ picked His apostles to create one of the biggest organisations human society has ever known, He did not chose natural leaders but, in today's terms, dustmen and farm labourers. In their lifetimes, these people, most of whom could not read or write, created international 'groups' using what would now be called network marketing techniques, including what we now call BOMs and sizzle sessions. If they could do that, without the use of cars, trains, phones, faxes, or overnight mail, every one of you can build the far smaller group you will need to create the income you want. It all depends on whether your purpose is strong enough.

However, let me stress that, although everyone has the talent to be a leader, only a very few will answer your call. But those few will have a dramatic effect on your business (see the chart on page 83).

Leaders can be made: they do not have to be born

In the early days of soccer there was little priority put on training, so the most talented players automatically rose to the top. The trouble was that there were nowhere near enough talented players to go around. Then clubs discovered that they could make a bunch of less talented *trained* players beat a team of more talented *untrained* players. Now, in every professional sport, a coach who is after a winner will every time pick a less talented sportsperson who assimilates training well over a more talented person who does not.

In business, too, it is very well proven that a less talented *trained* manager will go further than a more talented *untrained* manager.

If you do not consider yourself to be a born teacher and leader but are prepared to pay the price of making yourself one, and if you surround yourself with like-minded people, you can feel confident that you will build a vastly bigger business than those greatly talented leaders who build their hopes on the few untrained but talented 'natural leaders' who happen to land in their group.

Chapter 2

Staying On-Track: Reviewing The Basics

Before moving onto new ground, I would like to review some key points we learnt earlier in the S.T.A.R. Leadership Programme, to make sure that you do not Go Off-Track as a leader or teacher.

The Four Must-Do Activities For Success

The basic knowledge which every distributor needs is summed up in the **Four Must-Do Activities For Success:**

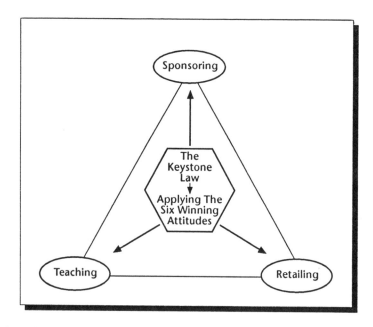

Another way of expressing The Four Must-Do Activities (which, if you think about it, means what you must teach every distributor) is:

- The basics of how the concept works
- The Six Winning Attitudes
- The day-to-day activities which lead to achieving what they want from the business:
  - How to sponsor
  - How to retail
  - How to teach others to do the same.

The Six Winning Attitudes

Applying the Six Winning Attitudes is the fourth Must-Do Activity which drives the other three. It determines *exactly* how well you sponsor, retail and teach and *exactly* how successful your business will be. Although they were well covered earlier in the Programme, I will pull them together for you:

- **Have Pride**, which means having pride in:
  - Your opportunity and your product
  - The industry of network marketing
  - Yourself
  - Your group
- **Have Drive**, which means you need a *Bulldozer Mentality* plus *Urgency In Action*
- **Be Patient**, which means:
  - Give the *Geometric Progression* time to work
  - When sponsoring or teaching, unfold at their speed, not yours
  - Give yourself the time to learn properly (give yourself a six months' apprenticeship)
  - Anchor legs properly before you leave them (I will cover this later)
- **Be Hungry To Learn**, which means:
  - Apply the **Training LLAWR** (Chapter 7, *Get Off To A Winning Start*)
  - Treat every situation as a learning situation

- **Have Focus,** which means:
    - Sponsor... Sponsor... Sponsor...
    - Retailing is the life-blood of the business
    - This is a teaching business
    - Focus on your purposes
    - Focus your actions on success (planning helps, see *Target Success!*)
    - Plan your business structure for security (I will cover this later)
- **People Buy People**, so take responsibility for the people who make your business:
    - Potential distributors
    - Distributors already in your business
    - Customers for the product.

In carrying out your job as a leader and teacher, I want to highlight three of the Six Winning Attitudes as being of outstanding importance to your success: Drive, Focus and Patience.

Drive and Focus

We are particularly interested in two aspects of Focus: *Focus on your purposes* and *Focus your actions on success by planning*.

The Winning Attitude of Drive together with these two aspects of Focus make sure that you keep going until you get to where you want, at the greatest speed of which you are capable.

But, more important, they create *momentum* and your first job is to get momentum into your group otherwise it will not survive. This does not mean that you need to be full-time but it does mean that you must accept that *you* are the **Momentum Generator**, the **Driver,** behind your group.

There are only two sources of momentum:
your *Drive* and your *Focus*

If you think about it, one way to phrase the purpose of this book is: *To make the results of your Momentum Generation, your Driving Force, as productive as possible.*

But the *danger* with learning techniques and theory is that they can dilute your sense of just 'getting on with it'. Drive and Focus become the casualties of bad training or leadership when the technique becomes more important than the results and, if you are not careful, the theory can stifle the talent. When I was a schoolboy cricketer, my results fell disastrously when an over-zealous sports coach made my batting technique more important than the purpose, to score runs. It was only when a new coach took over and encouraged me to open my shoulders that my run rate soared again.

So, before we get too deeply into how to be a winning leader and teacher, let's lay down two basic ground rules:

---

1. The results must always be more important than the technique. The only purpose of teaching and leadership is to get better results

---

2. No amount of knowledge will make up for any loss of Focus or Drive. **If the result of the S.T.A.R. Leadership Programme is that you lose even 1% of Focus or Drive, refocus your attitude!**

Many distributors have become high earners on the sheer power of their Drive and Focus, acquiring little knowledge of how to help others to succeed (see Motivator Michael, Chapter 3). That's not to say that they did much of a job for most of their people, but it does show that Drive and Focus are a great deal more important than knowledge. However, I challenge you to find the reverse: a distributor who lacked Drive and Focus but who became a high earner on the strength of their knowledge.

Patience

I am talking particularly about the need to have *The patience to give yourself the time to learn* how to lead and teach properly.

There is a tendency for new leaders to expect results yesterday. Impatience is a killer and it is a shame to see people drop out just because things didn't happen quickly enough. Yes, you do want to earn and you do want to earn *now*, but don't sacrifice your whole future on the altar of impatience, because there *is* no time-limit on success. This is not a sprint, it is a marathon. Do you want to be leading on the first lap or do you want to win? Network marketing has infinite patience with those who want to learn—it will wait for you to succeed. But it has no patience at all for those who choose not to learn.

The Keystone Law

The Six Winning Attitudes are themselves inspired by the **Keystone Law**, the fundamental truth about network marketing, which inspires all the Six Winning Attitudes and understanding which will be the key to your success.

In the light of your increasing knowledge, I am now going to update the Keystone Law for you:

How successful you become will depend on how many trained leaders and teachers you develop in your group

---

There is a danger that you may misunderstand what this definition of the Keystone Law is asking you to do. The rule that you cannot prejudge who will or will not succeed *still applies*. So you should not deliberately search for leaders and teachers. The only way you will find them is by doing what you are doing now: offering your opportunity to everyone and letting them self-select into who will succeed and who will not. As we saw in the last chapter, *everyone you show the business to has the potential to be a winning leader and teacher, so there is no need to prejudge.*

In other words, you must sponsor distributors, and lots of them, to find those few people who, not can be but *want* to be, serious leaders (everyone who sponsors has got to be a teacher).

On-Track—Off-Track

I refer constantly to On-Track and Off-Track so it is as well to remind you of what they mean. Someone is On-Track if they are:

• Putting in the time and the effort they promised

• Willing to Work With you and learn from you

• Willing to *apply* what you discuss with the right attitudes, particularly Drive and Focus.

Therefore, if someone is Off-Track, they are not putting in the time and effort they promised, or they are not willing to Work With you and learn from you, or they are not applying what they have learnt with the right attitudes, particularly Drive and Focus.

If a distributor Goes Off-Track, don't write them off. An amazing number of distributors do not come alive until months, or even a year, after they have signed up. So you should still keep them in touch with what is going on and make sure they feel that your door is open to them. Give them advice if they ask, but, apart from that, let them get on with it.

Avoid Dependency

Dependency means one of two things:

• That a distributor has learnt to depend on you to build their business for them

• That they are prepared to work only when you are Working With them.

The first situation is the result of bad tuition. It means that, in Working With a distributor and usually due to impatience, you are taking over jobs which they are capable of doing for themselves, and this develops into a habit of letting you do the work. To avoid this, ensure that you make the distributor do all the jobs their current expertise allows them to, and concentrate on teaching them to become capable of taking on more and more, until the point comes when they are doing all the work and you are simply there to advise.

The second situation means that the distributor lacks motivation. Unless something is found to motivate them, they will drop out. They are already Off-Track and, as a result, you should not be Working With them anyway unless your intention is to help them to sponsor some of their own contacts before they drop out.

The Theory of Duplication

The Theory of Duplication is the basis of all successful teaching. The more your distributors accept its importance and apply it to the way they act, the way they run their businesses and the way they communicate with others, the stronger your business will be. The Theory states:

1. People tend to do things in very much the same way as they were taught

2. People tend to teach others in very much the same way as they were taught themselves

3. People will copy what you do, not do what you say

4. Bad habits Duplicate more easily than good ones

5. Bad habits arrive unnoticed but depart with great reluctance. It is easier to change a good habit to a bad one than a bad habit to a good one.

Now that we have reminded ourselves of some of the basic concepts previously covered in the S.T.A.R. Leadership Programme, we can go on to discuss what leadership, motivation and training mean, and how they differ from each other.

Chapter 3

The Differences Between Leadership, Motivation And Training

People often get confused over the differences between leadership, motivation and training, and the three words are, as a result, often used interchangeably. The correct relationship is:

Winning Leadership =
Motivation + Training + Direction

So motivation and training are distinct parts of leadership and require different skills (I will come back to direction later in the book). Let's look first at:

What is a leader, what is a teacher?

We have already established that, to a greater or lesser extent, every distributor is a leader and teacher. But what is the difference?

A leader lights the way for their people; a teacher shows them what they must do to follow that path

---

A leader lays down the path which people must follow to get to where they want to go; a teacher shows people in detail how to follow that path. A leader shows the big picture, a teacher works with the practical details. Some people are good leaders, others are good teachers but few are naturally good at both. I will show you how to overcome that and win as both a leader *and* a teacher.

Those of us who lack charisma must build our businesses through professional teaching and leadership

Motivation is thriving in network marketing. There is something about the industry which allows charisma to blossom and most networks and large groups boast strong, compelling leaders and speakers. They exercise powerful motivational forces on their businesses.

Motivator Michael is one such person. In fact, he calls network marketing, 'the ultimate motivational business'. I asked him how he saw his role as a leader.

'That's easy,' he said. 'This is a very simple business. All it takes is the *right attitude* and *anyone* can succeed in it. My job as a leader is to point out to everyone what the opportunities are, show them what the right attitude is—and then motivate them to keep going!'

'What do you define as the right attitude?' I asked.

- 'First, have what I call a *Bulldozer Mentality*—in other words, just keep going whatever the obstacles are
- Then be *teachable.* Just do what I and the other front-runners do, and you will be all right
- Then be *credible.* Your contacts have got to *believe* what you say—if they don't, you'll never sign anybody up!
- Then, put in *massive action*! If you don't *Do*, you won't *Get*
- After that, all you need to do is: *teach other people to do the same.*'

'Is that all?' I asked.

'Yes, this business is incredibly simple:

- Just get a Contact List together
- Then show the product
- Show the business

- Invite your contact to a BOM (not all companies promote BOMs)

- Sign them up

- Then tell them to do exactly what you've just done...

'...and Bob's your Uncle—you're on your way to a fortune! Provided that people put in massive action and stick to sponsoring, retailing and teaching, that's it—they can't go wrong!'

'But they *do* go wrong, don't they!' I exclaimed.

'Yes,' Motivator Michael said. 'And I just cannot understand why people drop out so easily! Do you know, this is the *easiest* business I have ever been in? *Surely* it can't be any harder than what they were doing before and I *know* that, whatever else most of them do, it can't offer anything like the income, the freedom and the enjoyment that this business can. So just why don't they make it?'

Motivator Michael belongs to a group of people for whom network marketing might have been tailor-made, those with what can variously be described as having **charisma** or **magnetic personalities** or **natural leadership qualities.** They can find it relatively plain sailing because what sets them apart is a God-given gift to simply carry people along with them.

Motivator Michael tells everyone that his Drive got him to the top and, if people will copy what he did (which is what he means by being teachable), they, too, can get to the top. But he has got his equation wrong: he has left out his magic ingredient of charisma. I have seen many distributors try to copy the great motivational network marketeers and come badly unstuck because they can duplicate their Bulldozer Mentality, they can duplicate their sense of Urgency in Action, they can become equally focused, but no-one can duplicate their charisma. They either have it or they haven't.

That does not mean that you cannot build a major network without charisma—you most definitely can! But it does mean that,

---

Those of us who lack charisma have no choice but to base our success on providing professional teaching and leadership

---

I will show you how.

What is the difference between motivation and training?

- **Motivation** is what makes people take action, *but*
- **Training** is teaching people what to do when they take that action

---

People who confuse motivation with training think that, once they have motivated someone to act, they have also taught them *how* to act. Because of this confusion, very many 'First Step', 'Quick-Start' or 'On-Track' initial trainings are in fact more motivation than training. The result is that new distributors often leave all fired up ready to go, only to be brought up short when they think: *'But what do I do now?'*

If you take the comparison of a car, motivation provides the *fuel* to power the engine. But motivation is not the engine itself: the engine is your downline distributor. Nor does motivation fine-tune the engine—that is achieved by training. So to provide motivation without training is like filling up your tank with high-octane fuel without doing anything to ensure that the engine is tuned well enough to take it. If the engine is badly tuned, high-octane fuel is completely wasted on it. If the engine is very bad and the fuel octane high enough, it might well cause the engine to

*'I'm greatly motivated—
but to do... WHAT?'*

blow up—exactly what great motivators can do to some of their distributors!

Motivation without training—providing the high-octane fuel without the engine-tuning—is largely wasted because the only people able to benefit will be those who *already* have fine-tuned engines. That to my mind is not successful leadership, but it does in a nutshell describe the very great majority of network marketing training methods:

> **Most of the training in our industry only teaches the people to succeed who would have succeeded anyway. The purpose of the S.T.A.R. Leadership Programme is for you to help people to succeed who would not have succeeded without you**

Successful leadership is providing *anyone* who wants to succeed with the knowledge and support (Motivation + Training + Direction) to make it *irrespective of whether they already have a fine-tuned engine or not.*

To what sort of people do you have to give knowledge and support? Let's look at that in the next chapter.

Chapter 4

Your Only Path To Success—Your People

You have already seen that the secret of your success lies in understanding the Keystone Law or, more accurately, understanding what this law requires you to do, because the *only* ways you can turn it to your advantage are through leadership and teaching. They are the powers given to you to unlock the success of your distributors in order to create your own success.

To help people succeed, you need to know what makes them successful

In *every* field of human endeavour, and network marketing is no different,

---

It is ACTION plus ATTITUDES plus
KNOWLEDGE which brings people success

ACTION is the key because, without it, nothing happens: there *is* no success. Therefore the purpose of your teaching and leadership is to create action in your people.

But how much action people take, how determined they are in those actions and how successful those actions are, all depend on their ATTITUDES. So, as a leader and teacher, you should also work to help your people to develop the ATTITUDES which will make their actions as effective as possible. There are plenty of people around with Positive Mental Attitude (PMA) who do little about it, so their PMA is entirely wasted. Any PMA you help them to develop is also entirely wasted unless it results in action. But,

---

If attitudes decide how well your people *will* act, KNOWLEDGE decides how well they *can* act

---

So you also need to give them the KNOWLEDGE to help them to act as well as they can. Again, giving them knowledge which does not result in more action, more determined action or better action, is wasted knowledge. So, as well as the purpose of leadership and teaching being to unlock the power of the Keystone Law, we can say that,

---

The purpose of leadership and teaching is to create in your people the attitudes and actions they need for success, and to give them the knowledge to do that as well as possible

---

To help people succeed, you need to know what they want from you as a leader

The distributors in your group will fall into five categories:

1. Distributors who want to be led

These distributors are happier being part of a group in which they can see a hierarchy of strong leadership. Although this sounds contrary to the concept of network marketing, in which the appeal is supposed to be that everyone is their own boss, *the majority of distributors are in this category*.

Although self-employed, most of them would rather be treated as 'employed' in the sense that they are happier following instructions than giving them (having said that, few will Stay On-Track) and they are more comfortable having someone else make the decisions for them.

There is nothing wrong with this; indeed, it is just as well —can you imagine the chaos which would result if *everyone* wanted to lead? What is important is, if that is what these distributors want from you as their leader, that is what you must give them as a leader.

2. The 'top dogs'

These are the people at the very top of a company's network. If the group to which you belong is well established, they will be your top upline distributors. Just as few people in the world outside want to be the chief executive of a major corporation, so there will be only a tiny percentage of the total network who aspire to this position.

'Top dogs' are not necessarily cross-line of each other; one 'top dog' may be downline of another 'top dog'. Unlike top managers in conventional business, who see other aspiring 'top dogs' as a threat to their own position and therefore try to stifle them, *everyone* in network marketing is panting to attract such people because these are the people who will boost them to wealth! Indeed, the perfect position is to find and develop 'top dog' distributors in *every* leg of your business because you would now be earning a fortune for doing absolutely nothing apart, possibly, from having to qualify! (This is called *Passive Income*.)

3. First lieutenants: distributors who want to be seen as leaders but not as 'top dogs'

Some distributors in this category will have small groups, others will have very large ones—in fact, the largest of them may well have around 50% or more of a 'top dog's' business. Therefore, they qualify in their own right as big business-builders.

Like those in the first category, first lieutenants like to work in a structure. But, unlike those in the first category, they want to be part of the group's decision-making process. In conventional business, they would be on the board of directors, but would not want to be managing director.

They want to run their own group but entirely within the umbrella of a 'top dog's' group.

Some of the distributors in this category may be on their way to splitting off their group to become 'top dogs' in their own right. There is a confusion here because this is not the same as creating a *Breakaway* group. In many compensation plans, a distributor's group *automatically* 'breaks away' from their sponsor's business once they reach a certain position on the plan.

But this does not mean that a leader of a breakaway group will want to sever connections with the main group, unless they intend to be a 'top dog' in their own right. The practical difference is that a 'top dog' will want to set up their own trainings, possibly their own BOMs and also their own organisation for distributing training materials to their group (not all companies allow this). But a leader of a breakaway group who does not want to be a 'top dog' will continue to support their upline trainings, BOMs and training materials suppliers.

4. The talkers, not the doers

These are the sheep in wolves' clothing and, until you learn to recognise them, they can waste a lot of your time because they pay lip-service to the 'On-Track Route' but don't actually follow it.

Having said that, they are very supportive of you! They support meetings well. They turn out to events. They agree with everything the speakers say, even if they do not do it that way themselves. They will often help you, if asked. To some of them, network marketing is like a social life which earns them a little money. Others would like to be successful but never seem to get down to actually doing it; they usually drop out.

See if you can spot Jeremiah the Learning Junky because he is a very common character in network marketing; you bump into him at meetings. Jeremiah knows a lot about the business. In fact, you are so impressed by his knowledge of the business that you decide to find out more from him. Your conversation will go something like this:

'You obviously know a lot about network marketing. How long have you been in it?'

'About six months now.'

'Really? How big is your business?'

*'Well, I haven't actually **started** yet! I'm just getting all my facts right first.'*

Sorry, Jeremiah, but the only way you are really going to learn is by doing the job! And, much as you know about the theory, you have not yet learnt the practical effect of the Theory of Duplication—if you spend weeks or months learning about the business before you actually contact anyone, *so will your people!*

Network marketing junkies also come into this category but, unlike the learning junkies, they are not supportive of you. They have been in every network ever launched, sometimes several at once. They, too, know it all but use that to try to show your people how little *you* know and everything that is wrong with your product, your company and your compensation plan. All of these are excuses for their own failure but, because they talk with authority, they can dent the confidence of new distributors.

5. The 'lone wolves'

These are the distributors who are determined to 'do their own thing' or 'run their own show'. They are often highly motivated, hard working and committed to success but they rarely succeed because they insist on doing things their way, which usually means Staying Off-Track. These are some of the people who drown in the marsh on their way to the City of Dreams (Chapter 6, *Get Off To A Winning Start*), rather than turn back and ask you the way.

When we reviewed the Six Winning Attitudes in Chapter 2 I stressed the importance of *Patience—giving yourself the time to learn properly*. This is how you avoid being a 'lone wolf'. Some want to run before they can walk and therefore they do not give themselves the time to learn properly. Just this one thing makes them unteachable, but that is enough to make them pay the supreme penalty. Others believe that they know better than their uplines.

I find this the saddest group because they deserve better reward for their efforts but, if someone does not want to be teachable, you cannot make them so.

'Lone wolves' are very active and positive leaders, but they exclude upline help from their group, leaving them as the sole leader. This makes them major contributors to the drop-out rate because, when they fall out of the business, they leave a leaderless team who then also drop out.

Where do you fit into the team?

Leaving aside the 'lone wolves', you can see that every group organises itself into a leadership hierarchy, just like a traditional business. *Indeed, it is important that this is so because without it the teamwork, which is so important to success, would be impossible.* You cannot have teamwork without structure in your business.

What this means is that, although people are free to run their businesses in any way they see fit, it really is only the freedom to choose how they want to be part of the structure and the *team* and increase their chances of success, or, just like the 'lone wolves', to not be part of the structure and the team and almost certainly fail.

In which category do you see yourself?

Now you have a better picture of the role you are taking on, it is important that you understand the pitfalls involved. Just as everyone needs to be warned about 'The Pigs Around The Corner' which affect new distributors, you are more likely to succeed if you know what difficulties to expect as a teacher and leader. So, before we go any further, let's warn you about the 'Pigs' that may be lurking around *your* corner.

Chapter 5

As A Leader And Teacher, What Are Your 'Pigs Around The Corner'?

We covered 'The Pigs Around The Corner' for new distributors in Chapter 5 of *Get Off To A Winning Start*. The 'Pigs' I cover here are those which affect you as a leader and teacher. You should also warn your more serious distributors about these pitfalls.

So what are the 'Pigs Around The Corner' for teachers and leaders?

1. Getting people to make Get-Active phone calls!

Just about the hardest job you will find as a teacher and leader is to get your people to make enough Get-Active phone calls. When you come right down to it, these phone calls are the absolute key activity: if someone is making enough calls, their business will grow; if they are not, it will not.

If not enough sponsoring is going on for whatever reason, it boils down to not enough Get-Active calls being made.

The whole process of business-building has to start with phone calls. Unfortunately, most distributors find this by far the hardest thing to do.

After the Get-Active phone calls, most people find the rest of the sponsoring process—Two-to-Ones, meetings, trainings, retailing, teaching and even leading—easy in comparison. It is that first phone call which is the problem!

By and large, the more successful you are at getting your people to make Get-Active phone calls, the more successful you will be as a teacher and leader

---

There is a mass of detail to winning teaching and leading, but none of it is of much use to you or your group if they are not making enough calls. This book and the whole S.T.A.R. Leadership Programme needs to be looked at with that in mind.

2. If there is an Achilles Heel in network marketing, it is people not being teachable

When it comes to the need for tuition, the industry is hoist on its own petard. We constantly preach: *This is a simple business. Anyone and everyone can do it.* This leads people to the apparently obvious, but incorrect, conclusion that there is not much to learn, so much so that the majority put no priority on learning at all. *If it is so simple*, they think, *why bother?* No wonder we have a problem in getting people to read books, or go to trainings, or support meetings, or take advice!

When we say *simple*, what we mean is that anyone can learn what has to be learnt, we do not mean that there is nothing to learn. You will soon see from your own observation that the great majority have a great deal to learn and only a few have a little to learn. I have yet to meet the person who has nothing to learn.

The claim that the business is simple is only true if you Stay On-Track. *Simple* does not mean that you can do anything you like and still succeed in building a business; in fact, the business is devilishly difficult for anyone who

Goes Off-Track. If people find it so simple, why do they almost always drop out when they stray off the path?

The problem, as was said in The City of Dreams story (Chapter 6, *Get Off To A Winning Start*) is that,

---

If people *know* they do not know, you can teach them. If people *think* they know, you cannot

---

That story is very useful in getting across to your people how easy it is to Go Off-Track and what happens when they do.

Your answer to people believing that they do not need to learn is to teach your group to tell all potential distributors *before* they sign up that:

• There is a learning process to go through

• They are going to have to invest in training materials and trainings, *and*

• They are going to have to go through a learning curve.

Even so, not everyone will become instantly teachable, but the few extra who do will make a noticeable difference to your business.

The fact is that the business is only simple at its lower levels. The maxim, *Show the business, show the product and show others how to do the same* may work well enough to get going, or for part-timers or small business-builders, but anyone wanting to build a full-time business, possibly even of several thousand distributors turning over millions of pounds, is going to have to learn a few leadership skills (the only exceptions to this are the tiny number of natural charismatic leaders, see page 29). The leadership skills required may be very much easier to learn than the ones required by top managers in traditional business, but surely it is self-evident that one cannot build and control a business of any size without taking teaching and leadership seriously.

Once again, the answer is to warn your emerging leaders that this is so. If only a few take your advice and learn the teaching and leadership skills in this book, what a difference that could make to your business!

3. The potential for fast promotion causes a problem

One of the great attractions of network marketing is that you are 'promoted' as fast as you can 'make it'. But that also creates a problem of huge numbers of inexperienced leaders and teachers. In conventional business, promotion is hard to come by: getting one promotion in two years would be exceptional. Reaching the top of a corporate tree usually takes decades, if you ever make it at all! Although many potentially good leaders are held back by this system, the benefit is that people are given the time to grow gradually into the skills of teaching and leadership.

But, in the hothouse atmosphere of network marketing, distributors become instant teachers and leaders the minute they sponsor their first contact; in their first year they can have maybe six 'promotions' and may even reach the top of the 'corporate' tree. Add to this the fact that the majority of distributors have never had any previous management experience—and even if they have it is often totally unsuitable for network marketing—and it is easy to see why people finish up not being as good at leading and teaching as they can be. Even that is an understatement.

Fast promotion also breeds the belief that, because a distributor has built a business and can motivate groups of people, they must be a good leader and teacher. That does not necessarily follow. It may well be they have achieved this though personal charisma, and luck can also play a big part. Neither of these is duplicatable.

The industry has never come to terms with how to teach people to become good teachers and leaders *overnight*. Everyone realises how important leadership is and everyone does an excellent job of exhorting everyone else to teach their people; but there is not much point if you, and they, do not know what they are supposed to be doing. However, this is not an insuperable problem by any means and finding a solution was my vision behind creating the S.T.A.R. Leadership Programme.

4. Sponsors not accepting that they have reSPONSORbilities is a problem

It may seem obvious to you that, if someone asks a contact to join their business, they immediately accept a re*sponsor*bility to help that person succeed, but many of your people will not see it that way. Even if they do understand the importance of teaching and leadership, they will still not be able to discharge those responsibilities if they do not know how to go about them.

However there is also a reluctance to take up the responsibilities of leadership due to the widespread acceptance in business and throughout society that we are entitled to have rights or authority without responsibility. I am not going to argue the morality of this; I am only concerned about the problem it causes you as a leader, which is that many of your people will see it as 'OK' to sign others up and then leave them to sink or swim on their own.

Unfortunately, a tiny proportion of people in every network, those with charisma, will hit the top position in the compensation plan with this attitude. If you want to see a real live example, Motivator Michael in Chapter 3 exists in every mature network. This can make the problem worse when *you* are trying to promote good training, as these leaders create a misleading role model by proving that it is possible to reach the top with a 'sink or swim' mentality towards distributors.

These charismatic leaders will tell you that all you have to do is duplicate their approach and you will succeed. What they do not tell you is that:

1. Even they, had they used the principles of proper concern towards their people, would have reached where they are now a great deal sooner and more easily

2. Big though their businesses may now be, they could have even bigger, *and*

3. Unless you have charisma, you haven't a hope of emulating them.

This whole question of proper concern for your downlines is an aspect of Accountability, the 'A' of being an ACTTER (see *Breakthrough Sponsoring & Retailing*). The fact is that the average distributor in this great industry is simply shooting themselves in the foot unless they accept the re**sponsor**bilities which sponsoring brings, so let's develop this theme.

For God's sake hurry up and pull the trigger so I can get back to sleep

'A network marketeer who tries to exploit his downlines will only end up by shooting himself in the foot.'

> As a teacher and leader, you wield immense power. The minute you sponsor someone, you get the power anyway; it is up to you whether you exercise it well, or badly, or not at all

That power is the power to make below-par people average, average people good and good people fantastic. You have the power to turn failures into successes. That's one reason why I love this business! But, if you do not practise your craft well, you may, instead, turn potentially successful people into failures. People will fail *because of you*.

No one wants their downlines to fail, so someone who misuses their power as a teacher and leader is not going to do it deliberately unless he or she is a total fool. It is more likely the result of:

- A lack of understanding ('no-one explained to me how vital my role as a teacher and leader is to my people')
- Or lack of skill (they have not properly learnt what to do)
- Or inertia ('I can't be bothered to do it right')
- Or being unteachable.

The lesson is that it is well worth your while to take time out to explain to people why they should accept the responsibilities of teaching and leadership, because society may well have taught them otherwise.

Every distributor lost through bad leadership or teaching is also a distributor lost to you; every distributor handicapped by bad support is costing you sales and new recruits which, because of the Geometric Progression, has an exponential effect on your business (meaning an effect far worse than the cause would suggest).

For example, if your distributors average two recruits each, and just one of the new recruits fails to sponsor due to poor support, that has actually lost your business a total of *30 distributors* in just the 4 levels below them! Count them for yourself...

The high cost of bad leadership

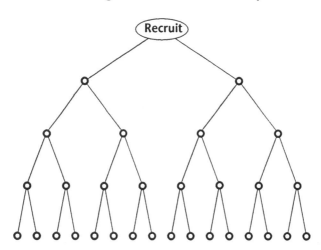

So, don't be afraid to make your views clear to a distributor who is letting down their group because they cannot be bothered to accept re*sponsor*bility for their people's success.

5. Human nature is a problem

Even if we solved all these problems, you will still be presented with the insoluble one of human nature. The biggest problem I hear from leaders is that their people will not do what needs to be done. Leaders often blame themselves for this, so it is with a sigh of relief when they discover that every leader suffers in the same way.

The fact is that, although *everyone* has dreams they would like to fulfil, few will ever do anything about it—that's human nature. As the story-teller in The City of Dreams story said, 'Had I offered them a magic carpet to take them there, *every single person in that audience* would have climbed aboard. But, left to themselves, few people in life will actually *do* anything about it.' (See Chapter 6, *Get Off To A Winning Start.*)

Every top distributor will tell you that, in every meeting and training, we are getting through to only a handful of people. The trouble is, we do not know which ones they are because only time will tell. So don't put impossible pressure on yourself by expecting to get through to a larger percentage! Concentrate instead on selecting the people who will do what they are supposed to do (I will show you how), 'home in' on them as the core and powerhouse of your group, keep going and you *will* succeed.

Even using the S.T.A.R. Leadership Programme, you and I will only reach only a few more people than the bad leaders and teachers, but that few will make an amazing difference to your business (see the chart on page 83). Our biggest successes, however, will come from the dramatic difference we can make to those few who *will* pay the price of Staying On-Track.

> *Hamish had fallen on hard times. His creditors were closing in on him. He realised that there was only one thing for it and that was to ask God to help him win the lottery. So he got down on his hands and knees and pleaded: 'Please God, help me. I'm in terrible financial trouble. I need to win the lottery. That's the only way out.' Nothing happened.*
>
> *Each day Hamish prayed, but still nothing happened. Each day he got more desperate until, one day, he cried out in despair: 'Please God! Do something! I'm desperate!'*
>
> *Back came an exasperated voice from on high: 'Hamish! But you've got to meet me half way! At least buy a ticket!'*

Many of your people will be desperate. Many will come to you for help but, like Hamish, they are not prepared to pay the price. God concentrates all the lottery winners on those who buy tickets and ignores the rest. You must do the same, but leave the door open for those who Go Off-Track because they may come back later. Unlike conventional business, your ticket office is never closed.

6. The need to attract leaders is a problem

This is one of 'The Pigs Around The Corner', already outlined in *Get Off To A Winning Start*. The Keystone Law means that the size of your business and the speed of its growth will be limited by the number of *winning* leaders in your business, so I am going to look at the issue again in more detail because it is a subject of supreme importance.

The problem is that the industry relies too heavily on that very rare breed of person, the natural, charismatic leader. There are virtually no leadership training programmes aimed at showing ordinary, motivated downlines how to become confident and effective leaders and teachers. This means that the only people who rise to the top are the natural ones.

I am not denigrating in any way the wonderful leaders to be found in every successful network. Many are good friends and no other business attracts so many exciting, uplifting speakers and motivators. It is very important to the health of our great industry that they are not replaced with the grey, characterless people who have taken over conventional business and in fact rule almost every facet of our lives.

The Motivator Michaels are the jewels in the crown of our business. The downside is that they have set the expectation of what leadership should be, but you can't rely on this type of leadership to build your business. Top upline leaders tell me that fewer than one in two thousand distributors have the natural leadership qualities to take them on a fast-track to the top without training. With few exceptions, they have amazing inborn gifts as motivators coupled with great Drive and Focus. The problem for you and the industry is that none of this is Duplicatable.

Unfortunately, at all levels of the industry, companies and group leaders do rather tend to hang around hoping to attract leaders with charisma. But, unless you are willing to rely on finding that one person in two thousand, you will need a way of turning ordinary people into leaders, and this is what the S.T.A.R. Leadership Programme is designed to provide.

Natural leaders will always have a role to play and, if you find one in your business, you should offer up thanks and give them special treatment. I will show you how in the section below. We are talking here not about undermining the natural leaders but about supporting their efforts by creating many more downline leaders and trainers to make them much more effective. We are also talking about applying the obvious truism that someone trained to be a leader and teacher will do a better job than the *same* person untrained provided, as I have said, that none of their Drive or Focus is lost in the process. Finally, we are talking about changing perceptions so that people realise that leaders do not have to be born: they can be made. The industry needs, and you will need, many more leaders and teachers than the current approaches give.

Even natural leaders need to take this problem seriously because, however massive their businesses, they would grow faster and with less effort if they relied less exclusively on charismatic downline leaders. In any business, not just in network marketing, charisma can actually replace the need to learn to do a job by the accepted rules. Therefore the danger, if you are a charismatic person, is to believe that, because you got there without conventional training, everyone else can do the same. Our interview with Motivator Michael on page 29 illustrates this very well.

Just as in the worlds of sport and conventional business, there is a wealth of people in network marketing who have the potential to reach the top level, *provided they are given the right training and support.* In *every* group the potential is there *right now* to make existing leaders better and to blossom budding leaders into flower.

7. Giving your leaders the wrong type of support is a problem

There are two sorts of leader: those with natural leadership abilities and those without. Decide which category any potential leader in your group is in, because you will need to train and support these two types of leader in very different ways.

The natural leaders

People with charisma pull everyone along behind them. They build big businesses quickly, usually breaking all the rules as they go. Though great at sponsoring and public speaking, they are often useless at anything else. You are unlikely to be able to curb their natural, ebullient natures, and nor should you try: the cure could be worse than the disease.

Although some combine great motivational ability with the patience to be a good teacher, many do not. So it is unwise to subject them to the straitjacket of formal training unless they have an appetite for it. Others are congenitally unable to plan but don't worry; as I said earlier,

---

Never make the technique more important than the results

A far better tactic is to recognise that such people are a big asset to your business. They could earn you a lot of royalty fast and will put a lot of *zing* into your motivational meetings. So why don't *you* take the responsibility of creating a team of teachers to give proper tuition to the people joining their fast growing businesses?

However, not all charismatic people succeed by any means. They still need Drive and Focus, two of the Six Winning

Attitudes—that is an inflexible rule which *no-one* can break. Therefore, if you have a downline who is squandering their rare gift of charisma through lack of Drive and Focus, you will be doing your business an enormous favour by using the techniques of the S.T.A.R. Leadership Programme to help them harness their charisma to determined and purposeful action.

Leaders without obvious leadership talents

Although training and structured leadership might stifle the tiny percentage of people with charisma, the complete opposite is the case with the vast majority. Very, very few of us are going to get to the top without good teachers and leaders to help us.

What we cannot do is get to the top both without charisma and without training. Yet that, I am afraid, is what most of us try to do.

We may also find that, to compensate for lack of natural talent, we need bigger helpings of Drive, Focus and Patience. Tackled in the right way, there is nothing to stop us building even bigger businesses than the most naturally gifted of the great network marketeers. Time and again, in the world of sport and business, people with Drive, Focus and Patience out-perform people with greater natural talents who do not use these essential qualities. There is no reason why the same should not apply to those of us in network marketing. In the next chapters, you should start to see why.

Part II
Be A Winning Teacher!

*In this Part, we concentrate on the **teaching** aspects of your job as a distributor, leaving the leadership aspects to Part III.*

*Let me remind you that, although we are talking about teachers, distributors **are** teachers and teachers **are** distributors.*

Much of the content here is new to the industry and some distributors, having built successful businesses without this much detail, will wonder if this is not unnecessarily complicating the job.

*Well, you only have to see the difference between a good distributor-teacher in action and a bad distributor-teacher in action to realise what a dramatic difference a few simple teaching skills **will** make to your business.*

*Yes, there are teachers to whom all this comes naturally but, for most, how to teach is **not** obvious. It needs to be understood that a bad teacher does more harm than good and will cause people to fail. But a good teacher can sometimes turn failure into success and will make those distributors who are willing to learn, even more successful even more quickly.*

The teaching techniques I show you here can be used by you and anyone in your business. But first, let's answer the question: what is effective training?

Chapter 6

What Is Effective Training?

What follows is an actual interview. It is so representative of the way the great majority of experienced distributors have been taught that I think you will find it of great value.

Trainer Timothy is a great believer in training. I asked him how he trains his group.

'Well,' he said. 'I have training sessions before each BOM. I train my distributors how to run their sizzle sessions. I spend a great deal of time on the phone telling people how to deal with situations or problems which crop up. Everyone knows,' he added with great pride, 'that I have an open door any time for anyone who wants help. And I send regular newsletters to all my group—do you want to see one?'

I nodded, and was impressed by what I saw. Timothy knew how to do a good newsletter; it was packed with good tips. I made a mental note to ask him if I could borrow some of his ideas for myself.

I asked, 'How do you train your new people?'

'Although I say it myself, we are pretty strong there. Apart from the Strategy Meeting which every new distributor has, where we go through all the basics involved in getting their business going, we have Fast-Start Trainings every Saturday, which is a good five hours' worth showing them exactly how to do their job. We even cover things like suggested phone scripts—and, of course, a very simple One-to-One: Show the Product, Show the video, Invite the contact to a BOM—you know the sort of thing.

'Then, once a month, we do a full-day Advanced Training which the serious distributors attend. On top of that, we run lots of occasional seminars on the basic topics: sponsoring, retailing—and most important of all—personal development. That's the real key! On top of that, we promote books, tapes and videos very hard.

'So you can see, our new distributors get a really good flying start. We tell them everything they need to know. If they can't make it after all that… well… they just haven't got what it takes!'

Timothy, like all good network marketeers, is very keen on training. I cannot fault him on his enthusiasm, his commitment and his determination to succeed.

Previously in the Programme (Chapter 15, *Get Off To A Winning Start*), we stressed that Working With is by far the most important form of training. Look carefully at what Timothy has said and you will notice that nowhere does he mention actually going out and Working With his people. But you must not blame Timothy. Following the Theory of Duplication, he is only following the example of his uplines, very few of whom go out and Work With *their* people. And you must not blame his uplines because, if there is one glaring weakness in our industry, it is the great lack of emphasis on Working With.

If the overwhelming majority of distributors think, as Timothy does, that *telling* people what to do is quite enough, there must be a general misunderstanding about what is really needed. So let's spend some time looking at exactly what you *should* be doing.

There are two sorts of training:
• On the job training or Working With
• Off the job or Arm's Length Training.

Working With means rolling up your sleeves and actually doing the job on site with your people. These are some of the activities you should do with them:

• Making phone calls to contacts
• Retailing
• Doing Two-to-Ones

- Carrying out Registration and Strategy Meetings with their new people
- Running or sitting-in on sizzle sessions for *their* group (as opposed to *your* group)
- Completing administration
- Planning their time and work
- Showing them how to developing the right attitudes in response to practical situations and problems.

Arm's Length Training means just what it says: covering the same above activities as Working With but *away* from the job—i.e., in group sessions or trainings, in newsletters, over the phone, even in what are confusingly called 'one-to-one' coaching sessions where you *talk* about the job without actually doing it together. If someone attends your sizzle session, you are giving them Arm's Length Training; but, if you attend theirs to help them to run it better, that is Working With.

If everyone did what they were taught to do at Arm's Length Trainings, *how much more successful would your group be?*

Here is the point that so few in the industry understand: *unless you Work With your people, there is little chance that what you teach will get done.* Left to themselves, people hardly ever do the job in the way it is taught at Arm's Length Trainings; they are much more likely to do so if they are *shown* on the job—and, even then, Constant Repetition (page 75) is needed to make sure they *keep* doing it in the right way. In other words, the effectiveness of intensive Arm's Length Training without Working With is marginal at best.

Looking purely at the *training* needs of your group, if you pay enough attention to Working With, you could entirely dispense with all *group* Arm's Length Trainings (many excellent salesforces in conventional business do) and end up with a far more highly trained group than is generally the case.

This may make you question the need for Arm's Length Trainings. *Individual* Arm's Length Trainings are important because you cannot be with everyone all the time, so you can 'fill in' with phone calls, newsletters and those confusingly called 'one-to-one' training meetings. *Group* Arm's Length Trainings are important for many reasons:

1. They get your people together on a regular basis. This is an important part of the business (as we saw in *Get Off To A Winning Start*) and a very important tool for generating motivation in your group

2. They are very useful in supporting *Working With*, provided that they are never done *instead* of Working With

3. They are an important part of *Constant Repetition*

4. The group discussions and the sharing of common experiences possible in Arm's Length Trainings are extremely valuable

5. They are indispensable to building teamwork, and network marketing is a teamwork exercise.

If you make two assumptions, you will not go far wrong:

- **That, without Working With, your people are just not going to do the job in the way they are taught at Arm's Length Trainings**
- **That the purpose of Arm's Length Training is only to support Working With, never to be used instead of it**

The upshot of all this is that, if you do not Work With your people, you are not a teacher. The whole S.T.A.R. Leadership concept is based on the assumption that you, as a teacher, Work With your people as much as possible. It is *all* designed to help you to Work With them more effectively.

Winning Teaching = Arm's Length Training + Working With

Now we know what is involved in training, let's take a chapter to look at what your aims should be as a teacher, because some of these may be different to what you might expect.

Chapter 7

What Are The Aims Of Being A Winning Teacher?

Contrary to popular opinion, the aim of teaching is *not* to increase the productivity of your distributors. If you are down on sales, the way *not* to increase sales is to try to teach your people to do more than they want to; that is for conventional business. By and large, in network marketing, distributors do what *they* want to do, not what you would like them to do.

If a distributor *wants* to increase their productivity, yes, you can help them to do so. That aside, if you want more sales, the only way is to sponsor more people.

Nor is the aim of teaching in network marketing to make people as good as they *can* be; not everyone chooses to stretch themselves in this way. The role of teaching is to make them as good as they *need* to be to achieve what they want from the business.

With these misunderstandings out of the way, here are the six main aims of being a winning teacher.

1. To build up distributor numbers more quickly by reducing drop-outs

Without proper tuition, most groups risk creating what I call a **Sponsoring Sieve.** This happens when the 'stream' of new distributors being poured into the 'sieve' of your business is being matched by those flooding out of the bottom, and your group effectively stops growing.

Actually, I prefer to think in terms of fine wine because distributors definitely are the fine wine of the business—difficult and time consuming to find with, just occasionally, a really good one turning up. Who would pour fine wine

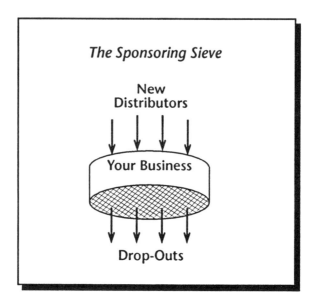

down the drain? Yet network marketeers do it regularly by sponsoring people and then not Working With them.

It is possible to keep your sieve full by pouring fine wine in so fast that it cannot escape quickly enough. But this is terribly wasteful and takes both exceptional sponsoring ability and sponsoring stamina. So, even if you are good enough to work in this way (and not many people are), do you have the stamina? If not, and you have to stop pouring for any reason, your sieve is going to empty fast.

The second consequence of sponsoring without teaching is that, because it is so wasteful, you will soon run out of warm market contacts. You are then forced into advertising, leaflet distribution, cold mailing, buying lists of names, visiting trade shows, going out of your way to 'pick up' strangers with a view to showing them the business, and any other ways you can think of to find new contacts.

A sponsoring sieve can occur with any size of group from two people to several thousand. It happens when the number of *effective* distributors simply stops growing. Yet it is so easy to stop! All you do is double-line your sieve to reduce the out-flow:

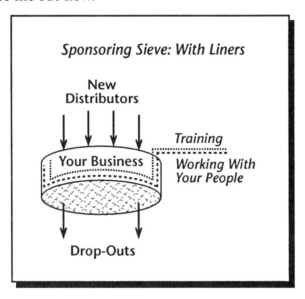

Leaders are often excellent at Arm's Length Training but that on its own, I hope you now accept, is a very leaky liner. The tough liner, the really important one, is Working With your people.

2. To help distributors get through their first six months!

The highest drop-out rate is during the first six months. If distributors get through that, they are much more likely to stick with you. During this period you are not looking at how to help them to succeed, *you are looking at how to help them avoid failure* because it is not the things they are doing right which will get them through this period, it is:

• Avoiding doing the wrong things *and*

• Learning to cope with problems

... which will get them through. The easiest time to cure a problem is early. Problems left unsolved are the ones which can grow to the point where they cause a person to drop out. So be alert for any sign of Going Off-Track and get them Back On-Track before it gets out of hand.

3. To help distributors to develop Patience

Patience, as you know, is one of the Six Winning Attitudes. Network marketing, as we saw earlier in the S.T.A.R. Leadership Programme, is not a sprint, it is a marathon. But it is a peculiar marathon in three ways:

• First, the winner is not the first person who crosses the line, it is *everyone* who crosses the line, no matter how long it takes them

• Second, no one knows how long the race is. We all run the race blind, so that you only know it is over when you cross the winning line

• Third, this marathon has obstacles. Because we all run the race blind, no one knows how many serious obstacles there are until they have finished the race. At each obstacle, distributors fail. If the drop out rate of distributors is between 75% and 90%, this means that between 10% and 25% cross the winning line. If we take the 10% figure, the race might look something like this:

How distributors drop out of the race

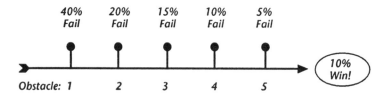

(Please note, these figures are for illustration only—and, of course, there are many more obstacles than five!)

What is so sad is to see some distributors dropping out at what might have been their last serious obstacle! The moral must surely be:

Never give up, because your next serious obstacle could be the last!

You will see that the drop-out rate is not even: it starts high and reduces dramatically with time. If you duplicate the culture of Working With throughout your group and, particularly, use the All-Out Massive Action Programme I will show you later in this book, you will smooth out this rate to your benefit because the longer people stay in the business, the more sponsoring and retailing they will do. It also means that the longer you can keep people in your group, the less chance there is that they will drop out.

4. To help those who drop out to sponsor more people before they do

You can never prejudge who will or will not drop out, or when. Bearing in mind that 75% to 90% will fail, (you just don't know which 75% to 90%), this is a huge resource lost unless you work as much of *everyone's* Contact List as you can as quickly as you can before they do drop out.

This may sound cynical but in fact it is not: the Urgency in Action this makes you generate into every new distributor's business greatly increases their chances of not dropping out, and may well result in you turning more people from failures into successes, which is the true measure of a great teacher.

Also, the more closely you Work With someone, the less chance there is of their people following them if they drop out. If you have not Worked With someone who drops out, they will take most of their group with them because their people have not established a rapport with you. In the final analysis, the longer you can help someone to stay in the business, the more time you are buying to help them to succeed. The longer you can help someone to stay in the business, the more chance you have of people coming into your business through them, one of whom could just turn out to be what we call a 'Star'—a high-flying distributor!

5. To help your distributors turn dreams into reality through the S.T.A.R. Success Pyramid

The aim of teaching is not just to reduce drop-outs, to help people get through their first six months and to avoid a 'knock-on' effect if a distributor does drop out. Important though those are, the positive side of teaching is to help those distributors who do stay to be as successful as they want to be. This is how you best apply the Keystone Law.

The success of every person, in whatever field of the professions, business, sport or art, has involved building, by accident or design, the same five stages. These make up **The S.T.A.R. Success Pyramid** (see over).

All five stages are necessary to the structure and the strength of each level is based directly on the levels below. That is why we show them in the form of a pyramid. To see how this works, take examples from your own life and see how, by accident or design, you went through these five stages to be successful. Then look at projects which were unsuccessful and see which stage let you down. You will also see how the stage which caused the problem weakened all the stages above.

The S.T.A.R. Success Pyramid gives you an easy-to-follow trouble-shooting chart; if a distributor is not succeeding, you will be able to trace the problem to one or other of the stages. Once you know the cause, you can seek a cure.

What is the point of having the fastest racing car in the world if a tiny fault stops it from finishing the race? One loose connection is all that is needed to bring a mighty piece of machinery to a halt and it is the same with a distributor's S.T.A.R. Success Pyramid. In the same way as an athlete's body is only as strong as their weakest point, the

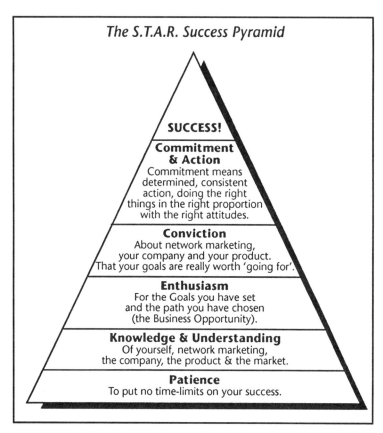

The S.T.A.R. Success Pyramid

SUCCESS!

Commitment & Action
Commitment means determined, consistent action, doing the right things in the right proportion with the right attitudes.

Conviction
About network marketing, your company and your product. That your goals are really worth 'going for'.

Enthusiasm
For the Goals you have set and the path you have chosen (the Business Opportunity).

Knowledge & Understanding
Of yourself, network marketing, the company, the product & the market.

Patience
To put no time-limits on your success.

strength of a distributor will be only as strong as their *weakest* stage, no matter how strong the other stages are.

Therefore, you need to stress to your people the importance of building each stage as solidly as possible. That is the only way to ensure that the S.T.A.R. Success Pyramid does not collapse into the rubble of failure.

6. To help distributors turn lessons into habits

As we said at the start, the *only* purpose of knowledge is to help people to *do* better. Until your knowledge as a teacher has been turned into, not just action but *habitual* action by the distributor you are teaching, your job is not complete.

Only when a distributor has turned a
lesson into a habit can you truly say, as a
teacher, that it has been learnt

The only way to turn lessons into habits is by Constant
Repetition.

According to the Theory of Duplication, the habits you
engender in the people you teach will be the habits they
will pass onto their people. Therefore it is vital that you
encourage the right habits!

Summary of the six aims of training

To recap, the six aims of training are:

1. To build up distributor numbers more quickly by redu-
cing drop-outs

2. To help people get through their first six months

3. To help distributors to develop the Patience they will
need to cross the finishing line

4. To help those who drop out to sponsor more people before they do

5. To help your people turn dreams into reality through the
S.T.A.R. Success Pyramid

6. To help distributors turn lessons into habits.

Now you know what your aims are as a winning teacher,
how do you carry them out? This is the question we turn to
next.

Chapter 8

As A Teacher, What Should Your Management Style Be?

How, as a teacher, should you treat your people? (if you want to be an *active* leader, there are several more aspects of this which are covered in Part III, *Be A Winning Leader*).

Be an ACTTER!

The ACTTER Formula was covered in Chapter 4 of *Breakthrough Sponsoring & Retailing*. To remind you, ACTTER stands for:

- **A**ccountability
- **C**onviction & Certainty
- **T**ell, not Sell
- **T**ruth & Trust
- **E**njoyment
- **R**espect

But being a winning leader and teacher adds a new dimension to the formula, which we will look at now.

Be Accountable to your distributors for helping them to succeed

We have a simple Code of Practice as network marketing teachers:

> It is *your* responsibility to show your distributors what to do, but it is *their* responsibility to decide what to do with it

Although you must do everything within your power to help people who are On-Track, if someone Goes Off-Track by not following your advice, your responsibility is discharged.

Conviction and Certainty

The confidence your distributors have in you plays a large part in their conviction that *they* can succeed. The only ones who can succeed *without* confidence in you are those few self-motivated individuals who are going to get to the top with or without you. The rest look to you to show conviction and certainty in your own ability to be a winning teacher and leader.

You must also show Conviction and Certainty in your distributors' ability to succeed if they Stay On-Track. If they do not feel that you have confidence in them, they certainly will not have confidence in themselves!

Be Team-minded

This is the only difference from the standard ACTTER Formula, as Tell, not Sell does not apply to teaching and leadership.

Remember one of the rules:

Network marketing is a *teamwork* exercise.
No-one ever succeeded in network
marketing by *not* going to meetings

Making people feel *welcomed* as part of the team is especially important when they first start. Everyone likes to 'belong'. Everyone likes to feel wanted. Everyone likes to feel special. More important than that, make each person feel a *valuable* part of your team—which, indeed, they are!

Meetings are vital to the team-building exercise. At meetings, you should circulate as much as you can among your people, particularly those who are new to your group, and make yourself known to the guests of group members.

Truth = Trust

The relationship between teacher and distributor is a very special one and has to be based on mutual Trust. Trust is worthless unless it is based on truth.

Enjoy the business! Enjoy meetings! Enjoy Working With your people!

Enjoyment is infectious. If you clearly enjoy what you are doing, your distributors will learn far more because they enjoy learning from you!

There is nothing more motivating than members of the group seeing their group leaders enjoying themselves! There is no better antidote to feeling down than seeing uplines enjoying themselves!

Respect your distributors' views

If you respect people's views, you will listen to them. Only by listening to what a distributor has to say can you be sure that you are 'pitching' your tuition in the best way for that distributor.

But also respect your distributors' efforts. A person may be doing a terrible job, but just remember that most new distributors are trying to do the best they can and anyone doing the best they can demands your respect.

So being a Teaching ACTTER is:
• **A**ccountability to your distributors
• **C**onviction & **C**ertainty
• **T**eam-minded
• **T**ruth = **T**rust
• **E**njoyment
• **R**espect

Being an ACTTER makes it easy for your distributors to trust you, believe in you and want to follow you. The better the ACTTER you are, the greater the loyalty your people will give you.

Learn to KISS and Play CUPID!

KISSing and playing CUPID were covered in Chapter 5 of *Breakthrough Retailing & Sponsoring* and the way I advised you there to apply these formulas to sponsoring and retailing applies just as much to your activities as a teacher and leader.

One reason why this is such a simple business is because it is very black and white: people are either committed enough to their own success or they are not, they either have the right attitudes or they do not, they are either teachable or they are not, they are either On-Track or they are not. As soon as you introduce grey areas, you are already complicating it for your distributors and you are no longer KISSing.

Because network marketing is a black and white business, it is easy to teach—provided you keep it black and white! Making sure that your people understand this is a black and white business requires a very straight-talking approach from you as both a winning teacher and a leader. Therefore, honesty and urgency are what distributors need from their leaders and teachers: honesty so that people know exactly how they stand in relation to their own success or failure (black and white); Urgency In Action to get the simple actions carried out.

Be Urgent, or be Patient?

I exhorted you to be Urgent in Action as part of Having Drive—but I also counselled you to be Patient. This sounds contradictory, yet both are part of the Six Winning Attitudes. When should you be one, and when the other? In practice, it is easy.

When you are teaching someone, be Patient: *Unfold At Their Speed; Unfold In Bite-Sized Chunks* (part of playing CUPID). But, as soon as it is time for them to put learning into action, show Urgency in Action. Then, back to teaching and Patience. Then, when it is time to put into practice what they have learnt, back to Urgency in Action. So, all the time you are Working With someone, you are swinging from one to the other:

When to be Urgent or Patient

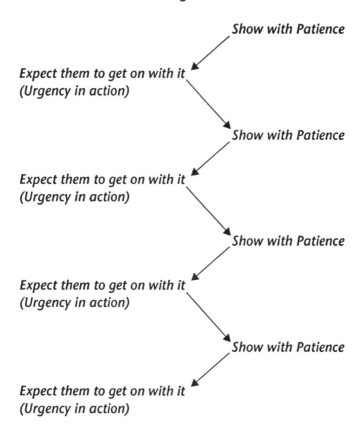

In the next chapter, I'll show you some simple teaching techniques to get your messages across. Most of these you have learnt already, possibly without even realising it!

Chapter 9

The Steps To Being A Winning Teacher

We will look briefly first at *what* you have to teach, before going onto *how* the teaching process works, then at how you 'lock' what you teach into people's work habits (Constant Repetition). Finally, we will define what makes a winning teacher.

People Buy People, one of the Six Winning Attitudes

When it comes to the way in which distributors should deal with other people, there are three topics you need to teach:

1. How to present *themselves* to contacts, customers and distributors already in their businesses

2. How to present the *product* and the *opportunity*

3. How to teach their people the same.

1. How should you teach distributors to present themselves?

By showing them how to become **ACTTERs,** which you can teach anyone straight from the text of Chapter 4 of *Breakthrough Sponsoring & Retailing.* To refresh your memory, the ACTTER Formula is designed to teach success through being a genuinely caring, trustworthy person who respects other people and enjoys what he or she is doing. It is the secret used by creative (as opposed to traditional) salespeople.

We saw earlier how you, as a teacher, should be an ACTTER.

2. How should you teach distributors to present the product and the business?

By teaching them to **KISS** and play **CUPID** which, again, you can teach straight from the text of Chapter 5 of *Breakthrough Sponsoring & Retailing*.

> The simpler you can make the path, the more the people who can follow you

---

These, again, are very simple formulas which you can teach to anyone.

3. How should you teach distributors how to teach their people to do the same?

First, teach them to use the ACTTER, KISS and CUPID Formulas when they are teaching their own people.

Then, use the Steps of Training

To apply the KISS Formula to teaching, in other words to make your teaching as easy to follow as possible, make sure that you take your people through the following **Steps of Training** in *every* teaching situation:

Explain:

- *What* to do
- *Why* do it and
- *Why* do it that way.

Show:

- *How* to do it.

Check:

- *Check* they understand (i.e. check absorption)
- Then *check* that it is working (i.e. check effectiveness).

You do not necessarily need to go through the first four Steps of Training in that order—that is going to depend on the circumstances. But you do need to develop the habit of going through *all* the Steps every time if you want your tuition to be as effective as possible.

You will notice from the Steps of Training that it is part of your job to make sure that your people understand what they are being taught, and then check how it is working in the field. You may think this is so obvious as to not be worth mentioning but, believe it or not, these are steps often neglected by even the best of professional trainers. I am the first to admit that I frequently go wrong on these points myself! It is very easy to assume that, because you know what you are talking about, the person listening must have taken it in or that, because they seem to be doing it, it must be working. Neither is necessarily so.

Time spent in tuition is completely wasted if, at the end of it, a distributor has not understood what they are being taught or cannot make it work. So we should constantly remind ourselves of the importance of these two steps by including them in our definition of teaching:

Winning Teaching = Explaining + Showing
+ Testing Absorption + Checking
Effectiveness

...and the best way to check absorption and check effectiveness is to observe your people as you Work With them in the field.

Coach Charles is an athletics coach. I asked him if he used the Steps of Training.

'Exactly so,' he said. 'There is only one purpose in training—nothing else—and that is to help athletes to compete (in other words to apply the *How*) as well as they possibly can. To do this, we see the Steps of Training as a circle with all the other Steps contributing *directly* to doing *How* better.

'Seeing the Steps in this way keeps *you* as a coach, On-Track. It helps you to check that anything you do is going

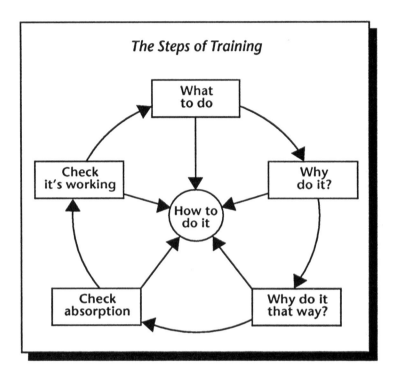

The Steps of Training

to help your athlete to perform better. If it does not, scrap it! But, of everything involved in training,

> Without question the most important thing is to Work With the athlete doing the job. All the valuable work is not in the classroom. It is *out in the field'*

The same applies to your distributors. See *yourself* as a coach, and you will not go far wrong.

Use Constant Repetition... Constant Repetition...

If you look again at our interview with Trainer Timothy, you will see that he is very strong on Constant Repetition, as indeed are all top distributors.

We said earlier that one of the aims of teaching is to create good habits of working: *Only when a lesson has become a habit in a distributor can you truly say, as a teacher, that it has been learnt.* Habits, good or bad, are *only* formed by Constant Repetition.

The *only* way to break a bad habit is by Constant Repetition of the good habit you want to replace it with.

Constant Repetition, although it can be boring, is the *only* way to make sure that a lesson becomes a habit. Once it becomes a habit with them, your distributors will constantly keep repeating the same message to their people— which is exactly what you want.

Constant Repetition is the only way in which slow learners and people with limited talent can learn

This is a business for all *only* if teachers use Constant Repetition. If they do not, they turn it into a business for quick learners or naturally talented people.

Constant Repetition is also the best insurance against people Going Off-Track, and that includes you!

It is very easy for a teacher to complicate things, to forget things or to give too much prominence to some things and not enough to others. Constant Repetition—re-reading books, re-listening to tapes, re-watching videos and attending meetings—will help you to Stay On-Track. This is why at least half of your Thirty-Minutes-A-Day habit (Chapter 7, *Get Off To A Winning Start*) should still be devoted to recapping.

The winning teacher: a profile of success

To summarise, a winning teacher is someone who:

1. Has sufficient knowledge and understanding of their subject

2. Understands a distributor's needs

3. Has the *Patience* (a Winning Attitude) to match their knowledge to a distributor's needs

4. Knows *how* to match their knowledge to a distributor's needs.

1. Knowledge and understanding of your subject. This will come if you have acquired the Thirty-Minutes-A-Day Habit. It will come if you accept the need for Constant Repetition.

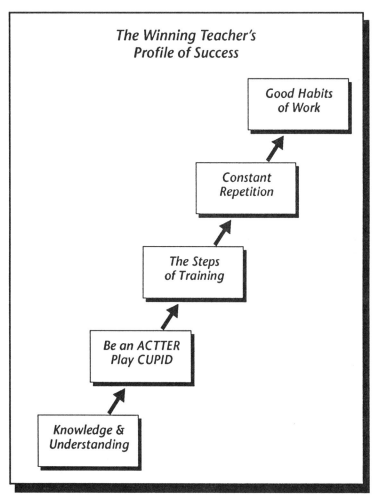

The Winning Teacher's
Profile of Success

Good Habits
of Work

Constant
Repetition

The Steps
of Training

Be an ACTTER
Play CUPID

Knowledge &
Understanding

2. & 3. Understanding a distributor's needs and Having the patience to match your knowledge to their needs. This will happen if you are an ACTTER and play CUPID.

4. Knowing how to match your knowledge to their needs. If you follow the Steps of Training we looked at above in every teaching situation, you will be matching your knowledge to a distributor's needs.

All these fit together to create what we call **The Teacher's Profile of Success**.

The most important teaching technique by far is Working With and I will devote the whole of the next chapter to this.

Chapter 10

The Basis Of All Teaching: Working With

I have already covered Working With extensively in the Programme and you should re-familiarise yourself with all that has gone before. But it is so fundamental to your job that it deserves a closer look.

Teaching people to succeed: the benefits of Working With

I expect you have already found how hard it is to get people to take action; yet nothing happens until they do! A way to make them take action is to Work With them. If you can show them results from the actions you take together, this may motivate them to keep taking action after you have gone.

I have already said in the Programme that, if you Work With people, they will develop at least five times faster than they will on their own. I also explained that you do not have to be experienced to Work With other people because two *inexperienced* people Working With each other will develop at least five times faster than each trying on their own, quite apart from the obvious courage and mutual support they can give each other during those critical early days. If you want to make someone as good as they want to be as fast as possible (which surely is the point of the exercise), Working With is the *only* way in which this can be done. But I think the most compelling reason is that Working With *opens the door for many more distributors to succeed.*

The great majority of your distributors will not succeed in network marketing on their own, but they have a chance if you roll up your sleeves and show them how

---

These are the people who, with their commitment, you can turn from failure to success, by far the most rewarding achievement there is in training and leadership! It really is the *only* way to give each person the best chance they can have.

Working With means that doing the job is teaching it; teaching the job is doing it

The concept of Working With is based on the principle that doing the job and teaching it are inseparable, so much so that I said in my book *Target Success!*, 'Your Monthly Diary should *never* show you working on your own. *Every entry* should be Working With—upline, downline or crossline.'

Working With produces a massive payoff for your business

But Working With has other benefits. It reduces drop-outs because, if you Work With someone closely, they are far less likely to drop out than if they are working on their own.

Just a tiny reduction in drop out rate due to Working With your people can have a truly massive payoff in terms of how your business builds. Let me give you an example (see chart on page 82) and, to keep it simple for the purposes of illustration, I am going to make the following assumptions:

• That we start with a group of 100 people

- That the average drop-out rate of your group is 90% (drop-outs vary generally between 75% and 90%). So, out of every 100 distributors sponsored into your group, 90 will drop out. This means that 10% (or ten out of every 100 sponsored) are actively sponsoring and retailing at any given time

- That your *active* distributors sponsor an average of ten people during each sales period

- This chart does not represent any particular time-period. It could be one year or ten years—for the purposes of what we are talking about, it does not matter.

This means that, in Period 1, you start with 10 active distributors, being 10% of your group of 100 people.

Those active distributors sponsor 10 people each, making 100 new distributors in all. From those 100, 10% or 10 *new* active distributors will emerge. Add those to your original 10 active distributors, and you now have 20 active distributors in total your group.

In Period 2, your 20 active distributors sign up 10 new people each, making 200 new distributors in all. From those 200 new distributors, 10% or 20 new active distributors will emerge. Add those to your original 20 active distributors, and you now have 40 active distributors in total in your group.

In Period 3, your 40 active distributors sign up 10 new people each, making 400 new distributors in all. From those 400 new distributors, 10% or 40 new active distributors will emerge. Add those to your original 40 active distributors, and you now have 80 active distributors in total in your group.

In Period 4, your 80 active distributors sign up 10 new people each, making 80 new distributors in all. From those 800 new distributors, 10% or 80 new active distributors will emerge. Add those to your original 80 active distributors, and you now have 160 active distributors in total in your group.

In Period 5, your 160 active distributors sign up 10 new people each, making 1,600 new distributors in all. From those 1,600 new distributors, 10% or 160 new active distributors will emerge. Add those to your original 160 active distributors, and you now have a total of 320 active distributors in your group.

In Period 6, your 320 active distributors sign up 10 new people each, making 3,200 new distributors in all. From those 3,200 new distributors, 10% or 320 new active distributors will emerge. Add those to your original 320 active distributors, and you now have 640 active distributors in total in your group.

The chart of your group growth of active distributors will therefore look like this:

Group growth with 10% of independent distributors (IDs) becoming active

Period	1	2	3	4	5	6
A	Active IDs at start of period	10	20	40	80	160	320
B	They sponsor 10 new IDs each	100	200	400	800	1600	3200
C	10% of new IDs become active	10	20	40	80	160	320
D	Active IDs at end of period (A+C)	20	40	80	160	320	640

Now, let's see what happens if, by Working With your people, you reduce your drop-out rate by just 1%: from 90% to 89%. First, your percentage of *active* distributors will go up not by 1%, but by *10%* (or from ten to eleven out of every 100 sponsored).

At first sight you might think that this 1% reduction in drop-outs will give you a 10% increase in sales. But a network marketing business does not grow in a straight line, it grows on a Geometric Progression, and the results of that can be amazing:

Group growth with 11% of independent distributors (IDs) becoming active

	Period	1	2	3	4	5	6
A	Active IDs at start of period	11	23	48	100	210	441
B	They sponsor 10 new IDs each	110	230	480	1000	2100	4411
C	11% of new IDs become active	12	25	52	110	231	485
D	Active IDs at end of period (A+C)	23	48	100	210	441	926

To make this conservative I have said that, despite your better support, each active distributor is still only producing ten new people at each step. Even so, after six steps, you have finished up with 286 extra active distributors, an increase of 45%!

Not bad, for such an apparently insignificant increase as a 1% reduction in the level of drop-outs!

Some people may feel this comparison is unrealistic because they believe that active distributors are being required to sponsor ten people off their own warm market lists in every sales period. Not so. If you follow the S.T.A.R. Leadership Programme, each or your active distributors will be sponsoring from the Contact Lists of the 89% or

90% who drop out (of course, *before* they drop out!), as part of Working With them. If you feel that this figure is still too high, drop all the sponsoring figures to five and you will see a similar pattern.

This chart is the best way I know to get the message across that Working With is well worth doing even if the results seem insignificant at first. Just as with business-building, you need to fully understand the value of Patience in your teaching to give the Geometric Progression time to work.

How to introduce Working With to your group

But here comes the problem: it is very difficult to get your people to Work With as a consistent habit, and to make this an accepted culture throughout your group. It is going to take Constant Repetition to keep them doing so, despite all the compelling arguments in favour of Working With, and even though there is *not one* argument against. The most common objection is about wasting time in Working With the wrong people—but I will show you how to avoid even that.

If you already have a group in which Working With is not the accepted culture, you are going to find it very hard to change that bad habit. Remember the Theory of Duplication: *It is easier to change a good habit into a bad one than a bad habit into a good one?*

There is a slogan, *It is easier to give birth than to raise the dead*, meaning that it is very much easier to teach new people than to retrain existing people. So you will have better results if you concentrate on introducing the concept to new distributors because, unless they have already been in another network, they will not yet have developed bad habits.

But don't neglect your existing people, because converting just one will make the exercise worthwhile and, if others see the results which that person can generate, they may follow suit. I suggest that you call your people together for a focused discussion on the subject. You will find enough material in the Programme to date (including *Target Success!*) to do a red-hot presentation but, because this is so important to your success, if you are having a problem please contact me through Insight Publishing (page 249).

Experienced distributors should also Work With each other!

Working With does not necessarily have to consist of a new distributor going out with an experienced upline or two inexperienced distributors going out with each other. It could be two experienced distributors going out together to compare notes—this is an *enormously* valuable and much under-rated exercise. The distributors do not even have to be in the same paylines for both of them to receive great benefit.

What kind of teacher will you be?

If you wanted to be taught how to drive a car as well as possible in the shortest possible time, which instructor would you choose:

1. One who spent as much time as possible in the car with you and encouraged you read books and go to lectures

2. One who spent as much time as possible in the car with you, but did not make you read books and go to lectures

3. One who only came out with you for a couple of quick trips, then taught you by phone and got you to read books and go to lectures

4. One who would never get into a car with you, did all their tuition by phone and got you to read books and go to lectures

5. One who did all their tuition by phone and didn't encourage you to read books and go to lectures?

I wonder if anyone would not agree that the best order is 1, 2, 3, 4, 5? Yet the typical network marketing situation is 3,

4 or 5 with, a long way back, 1 (2 hardly exists. People who spend as much time as possible doing the job with you tend to be great believers in you soaking up knowledge in any other way you can. These are the *only* people with a *genuine* Hunger to Learn).

I hope I have convinced you that 1 really is the only teacher to be and the only person who can genuinely call themselves a great teacher!

Now you know the techniques you can use to make yourself a winning teacher, let's answer the next question—on whom should you choose to exercise your new-found skills? One thing is for sure: you do not want to waste your valuable talents trying to turn sows' ears into silk purses!

Chapter 11

How Do You Choose Which Distributors To Work With?

The short answer is—to begin with, you don't. Remember the rule: *It is impossible to prejudge who will succeed and who will not*, so you give everyone the same and equal chance when they start, and then let them self-select into those who value your advice and act on it and those who do not.

But, until you learn from your own experience that prejudging is a waste of time, I have to be honest and admit that it is exceptionally difficult to avoid, and this makes it very easy to concentrate on the wrong people. So I'll show you how to choose the right people to Work With.

People tend to split into two categories: talkers or doers

The trouble is that logic suggests it should be possible to prejudge: and logic further suggests that you should lean towards the ones with the 'right' background or the 'right' experience or the 'right' Contact List or the 'quick' learners.

Or you might assume that the people who have obvious leadership qualities, who project themselves the best or who 'talk the best act' are going to be your best bets. But,

---

'Talking a good act' is not the same thing as doing a good job. So forget the good talkers and look for the good doers

---

Anyone can *talk* about what they are going to do. That is easy. It is much harder to actually go out and do it. You will find at meetings that good talkers often overshadow good doers, so you need to be able to look past them to spot those often quieter people who are going to beaver away in your business.

Although you need to learn to value the doers rather than the talkers, there are, of course, people who are both good talkers and good doers. With them you will have the best of both worlds!

If you cannot judge by the 'obvious' qualities I mentioned above, what can you look for? As a serious winning teacher, the *only* things you should look for in a new distributor are:

- Do they want to succeed in network marketing?
- Have they a Hunger to Learn—one of the Six Winning Attitudes?
- Will they apply what they have learnt?

These are the only attributes you, as a teacher, are looking for because *they are the **only** three things which you cannot teach!*

Everything else a distributor needs, you can teach:

- *Anyone* can be taught to do the Get-Active phone calls
- *Anyone* can be taught to do an adequate Two-to-One
- *Anyone* can be taught to retail
- *Anyone* can be taught to show the business
- *Anyone* can be taught the right attitudes
- *Anyone* can be taught to teach *anyone* else to do any of the above.

The only things you cannot teach are:

- The wish to choose network marketing as a career or occupation
- The willingness to learn, *and*
- The willingness to apply what they have learnt

... to people who do not want do so—no matter how 'right' their background, how 'right' their experience, how 'good' the people on their Contact List or how quick a learner they are.

So, when you are deciding who to Work With, choose only those who Stay On-Track (see Glossary) because, while people are On-Track, you have a re**sponsor**bility to teach them. If they Go Off-Track, your responsibility is discharged. In that case, leave them to their own devices, but keep the door open for them to return.

Spend your time with your performers

The *80/20 Rule* applies to training just as it does to many other things. But, in conventional business, it is the wrong way round: sales trainers spend 80% of their time with the bottom 20% of their salespeople. *So they spend the bulk of their time with their **non**-performers.* Put like that, it sounds crazy but in fact that is the only way the traditional system will work.

However, the biggest kick for trainers comes from being with people who *want* to learn, not with those whose response to tuition is to do just enough to get by:

'I'm here to show you how to make the best use of your considerable talents!'

I'm here to learn how to do as little as possible to get by...

In network marketing, the complete opposite rule should be applied. We should spend 80% our time with distributors who *want* to learn and only 20% with those who do not. That's much more satisfying!

The other very big difference is that, whereas in traditional business the job of training is to make people achieve what the *company* wants out of them, in network marketing, your job as a winning teacher is to help people achieve what *they want for themselves*. That, too, is much more satisfying.

What should you do about the slow learners or those who lack confidence in their ability?

Welcome them all!

Give me one person who learns, no matter how slowly, rather 100 more talented people who do not. My experience in both sales and network marketing is that slow learners or less talented people are very often those who come out on top, *provided that they have Drive and Patience*. As we said earlier, there is nothing in network marketing which cannot be learned by *anyone*, so long as they give themselves the time. Constant Repetition (see page 75), which is important for everyone, is the real key to teaching slow learners or less talented people.

Slow learners are less likely to forget

If a distributor has to struggle to learn something, isn't it more likely to stick in their brain? *Easy come, easy go* applies just as much to gaining knowledge as it does to anything else.

Slow learners tend to have more patience

They say that good teachers make the best distributors and Patience (one of the Six Winning Attitudes) is essential to good teaching. Slow learners or less talented people, having had to struggle themselves, are more likely to sympathise with someone else who is struggling.

Slow learners are much more likely to Stay On-Track

People with quick minds or those with talent are more likely to Go Off-Track by trying to invent short-cuts or 'better' ways of doing things, or to generally complicate the issue. Slow learners or less talented people are more likely to go unquestioningly down the proven success path you have set out for them. This of course puts an extra onus on you to make sure that you have prepared the right route for them.

Where slow learners or less talented people are concerned, there is an extra responsibility on you to make sure that you set their minds at rest

You can do this very effectively by following this six-point procedure:

1. Explain that there is *nothing* they can't learn, *if they give themselves the time*

2. Point out the advantages we have just been discussing to show how they will eventually come into their own— perhaps after so-called 'cleverer' people have dropped out

3. Get across the message that if, by perseverance, they create a good business with a high income when the 'clever' people have dropped out, *who is the smarter person then?*

4. Make it clear that *This is not a sprint, it is a marathon.* Would they rather be in the lead at the end of the first lap, or win the race? Everyone who crosses the line by achieving what they want for themselves from life is a winner and, in marathons, people who set off too fast frequently fail to reach the line

5. Encourage them to *Put no time-limits on success.* At the end of the day, there are only those who make it and those who do not, so they must not worry if other people appear to achieve more quickly than they do. Explain that every experienced network marketeer has seen the high-flyers come charging in, quickly building huge balloon businesses and filling other, slower moving distrib-

utors with self-doubt. But, a few months down the road, where are they then? Gone, while the more tenacious distributors are still there building cannonball businesses, slowly but solidly

6. Finally, put in the confidence booster that you are so sure they are going to succeed that you are prepared to give them a lot of your very valuable time. You will help, advise and, most important of all, *Work With* them every step of the way—provided, of course, that they Stay On-Track.

To summarise: work hard for those who work hard for themselves

Although you cannot decide who to spend your time with by prejudging, you can make sure your time is well-spent by committing yourself to those who Stay On-Track. This is easy if you get people to agree to what they have to do, in other words, who agree to *Focus their actions on success.* Then you can judge if they are On-Track or not. I'll show you a more sophisticated way to get this agreement in Chapter 17.

Having chosen the right people to Work With, how much time should you give each? We'll discuss this in the next chapter.

Chapter 12

How Much Tuition Will A New Distributor Need?

The amount of tuition different people need varies enormously. In this respect, you will find your distributors come in with three different attitudes to sales:

- Those who want to *Sell the deal*
- Those who are ACTTERs—they want to help people
- Those with no idea what to do.

Those who want to 'Sell the deal'

These are generally traditionally trained salespeople, thrusting entrepreneurs and people with positive, outgoing, perhaps competitive, personalities.

It is common for new distributors to prejudge such people as the ones to 'home in' on as their first recruits. You will need to warn them not to do this because people who set out to *Sell the deal* are, if anything, less likely to succeed. As we discussed in Chapter 8 of *Breakthrough Sponsoring & Retailing, Selling the deal* leads to disaster. So distributors who do this need to be taught to 'back off'. Instead of 'selling', they will need to learn to 'show', 'invite', or 'share' (whichever word you like to use).

It is particularly difficult to teach traditionally trained salespeople to do this because you are trying to change them from a totally different philosophy of selling which may have become a deeply ingrained habit and which breaks just about every rule of the ACTTER Formula. The trouble is that, if they do not learn, they will in turn treat their distributors as traditional salespeople and the attempt to sell rather than show will duplicate down their leg of *your* business—usually with disastrous results. So I would not spend too much time on them unless they are prepared to learn to *show* rather than *sell*.

However, if you *can* convert an experienced salesperson to being an ACTTER, you are likely to have a real 'Star' in your business, partly because they will find that showing is much easier than the selling they are used to, and partly because they can then use their previous experience and skill to advantage.

The ACTTERs; those who want to help people

Among others, creatively (as opposed to traditionally) trained salespeople come into the ACTTER category. They need very little tuition because they are already very close to the network marketing way of doing things:

> Creatively trained salespeople are taught to make friends of their customers whereas distributors in network marketing are taught to make customers of their friends

... As you can see, not much difference. Both techniques mean learning to *Show not sell*; so creative salespeople have already, without knowing it, learnt to apply the *ACTTER Formula*. This does not mean that they are any more likely to succeed, but they will need less tuition.

Also coming into the ACTTER category will be helping professionals such as nurses, teachers and social workers, and people who have been properly trained to deal with the general public: receptionists and telephonists, retailers and retail assistants, and so on. They will quickly learn how to present themselves, the product and the business.

Those with no idea what to do

These will be the majority of your distributors but I think you have already gathered that this is not a disadvantage! You need to remember that *95% of network marketeers nei-*

ther are, **nor will want to be,** *trained salespeople in the traditional sense.* They are people not used to dealing with the general public and who may find the whole business of showing the product and the opportunity very difficult to start with. Less obvious examples of people who may have no idea what to do are educated, intelligent people like professionals, some company directors, managers and technicians, who have not learnt how to deal with people in the right way.

Long experience proves that people who come in with no idea what to do stand every bit as much chance of success as those in the two earlier categories, because they are often the most teachable ('If people *know* they do not know, they can be taught; if people *think* they know, they cannot'). People who have been trained or who have experienced success in business or sales can have so many preconceptions about how things should be done that they have become unteachable.

Two areas of communication require specific tuition: the Get-Active phone call and the Two-to-One

1. The Get-Active phone call

Getting people to make Get-Active phone calls really is the big issue in network marketing.

We covered the basic Get-Active phone call in Chapter 11 of *Get Off To A Winning Start*. The more advanced technique, the Reactive phone call, was covered in Chapter 13 of *Breakthrough Sponsoring & Retailing*. You can teach straight from the texts of those two chapters.

You should not involve a new distributor in Reactive phone call techniques until they are confident with the basic phone call.

The fear of phoning is made much worse by people not *Focusing on their purposes.* The purpose is to achieve their goals; actions like difficult-to-make phone calls are essential to achieving that purpose. If they forget to focus on their purposes, the phone calls become an end in themselves and therefore much harder to make.

You may find it helps some people to read their **Goals Sheet** just before each phone call, or to prop a photograph of some important person or desired object by the phone, thus getting them to concentrate on their purpose and away from their reluctance to make phone calls.

Don't forget the Chicken List!

The Chicken List is the hottest part of anyone's warm market! Assuming that each distributor averages 10 people on their Chicken List and that these are their hottest contacts, as a leader you cannot afford to throw those contacts away. If you do, with only 100 people in your group, already 1,000 of the best contacts are not being approached!

The subject was covered in Appendix II of *Breakthrough Sponsoring & Retailing*. But I find the two most effective cures are to remind downlines that, if they do not approach a contact, someone else will and how will they feel if that person signs up with another distributor or, second, to approach people on their Chicken List in the first instance only as retail customers or as sources of referrals.

2. The Two-to-One

We looked at the steps of the basic Two-to-One in Chapter 12 of *Get Off To A Winning Start*, followed by the more sophisticated Reactive Two-to-One in Chapter 13 of *Breakthrough Sponsoring & Retailing*. These will allow you to gradually wean even the most inarticulate, inexperienced and slow learners into becoming competent at showing the business.

Again, don't introduce a new distributor to Reactive techniques until they are comfortable with the basic approach. The important thing is to play CUPID: let people learn at a pace at which *they* feel comfortable. To start with, you can conduct the whole Two-to-One yourself. The system then allows you to *gradually* give new distributors more to do in line with their increasing confidence. If you rush them, you risk losing them and you will be teaching them badly. But bring them in carefully and you may finish up with 'Stars' who have the patience to become winning teachers themselves.

You will greatly accelerate the learning process if you show new distributors how to use a **Presentation Folder** in Two-to-Ones (Chapter 5, *Breakthrough Sponsoring & Retailing*).

How many Two-to-Ones should you do with a new distributor?

Let's deal with the theory first, and the theory is: *Do as many as are necessary!*

With people who want to 'sell the deal', you will only need to do a few before they either grasp the 'showing' rather than 'selling' approach or prove to be unteachable. If they prove to be unteachable, don't waste any more of your time.

You will need to do even fewer Two-to-Ones with *creatively* trained salespeople because they are already used to presenting both themselves and their product in a network marketing way. They are already following the ACTTER Formula without realising it.

The normal practice with uplines, if they do Two-to-Ones at all, is to do just enough with a new distributor to allow them to go out on their own. Then, in their haste to cram as many new distributors into their business as they can, they go charging off to rush someone else through a couple of Two-to-Ones.

It may seem that judging them ready to go out on their own is the right yardstick. *But it isn't.* Remember that this is a *teaching* business. Although a new distributor may be good enough to go out on their own,

---

Do they know enough yet to teach their new distributors as well as *you* could teach them?

It is not your standards and techniques, but the standards and techniques of your new distributor, which will duplicate down *their* leg of *your* business. Looked at in this way, are you still satisfied that your new distributor has learnt enough to teach your people properly?

So the main purpose of doing Two-to-Ones is not to make sure your distributors know how to show the business. It is to make sure that they teach their people to show the business—and that *they* teach *them* to teach others—to at least the same standards as yourself. Only in this way can you ensure that your standards and techniques reach undiluted to the bottom of your business

---

On this basis, it is hard to think that even the best new distributor would need fewer than five Two-to-Ones. Someone who is not used to dealing with the public and is a slow learner, and perhaps lacks confidence as well, will need... how many?... As many as it takes!

That is the theory. The reality is that a good and conscientious teacher can almost never do as many Two-to-Ones as they would like with a new distributor. The minute the new distributor has two distributors in their group, you are going to have to let them Work With one while you look after the other, or someone else you need to Work With. The option of *Three*-to-Ones (you taking the new distributor *and* their new downline along to meet a contact) is not acceptable: *Three*-to-Ones are really a bit much for most contacts!

This makes it very important that you talk through, by phone or in person, *every* Two-to-One an inexperienced distributor makes with their people, and every session of Get-Active phone calls they have with their downlines, as well as discussing in detail the advice they are giving to their people.

Your inexperienced distributor's downlines, too, will have to stop Working With your inexperienced distributor for the very same reason, when *they* have people in their group whom they have to Work With. As a conscientious teacher, you will also have to talk through the same three topics (Two-to-Ones, Get-Active phone call sessions and the advice they want to give to their people) with them, too, until the original distributor is experienced enough to take over.

Now we, as teachers, are getting moving. So let's see in the next chapter how you can Fast-Track a new distributor into action and early success.

Chapter 13

How To Fast-Track New Distributors

I said earlier that one of the aims of teaching is to help reduce drop-outs. People often drop out either because either they are not fast-tracked into action quickly enough or because, due to poor upline support, they are allowed to Go Off-Track right at the start. In this chapter, I will show you how to avoid four significant causes of failure.

First, lack of early results makes people drop out

Urgency in Action applies just as much to how you start new people as it does to how you act in your own business. There is nothing better than experiencing *success in action* for making new distributors want to do more and better. In the next chapter, I will show you the very best way to apply Urgency in Action to a new distributor's business.

> A little personal success is better than one thousand words or one hundred examples of other people's success

---

The worst delay can occur at the beginning. No matter how long it took them to make up their minds, as soon as people sign up they want to get going. Then you make them wait one or two weeks while their starter kits and any samples they have ordered arrive!

The quickest way to get people started is:

- Have spare starter kits and suitable samples on hand to get them going straightaway

- Arrange the earliest date you can for their Strategy Meeting (Appendix II, *Breakthrough Sponsoring & Retailing*), giving only time for stock and administration orders to arrive from head office

- Get them booked into the first available training

- Get them to your next sizzle session

- Take them to the next BOM (if your company promotes them)

- Lend them a book, tape or video—but do not overdo this! Remember: *Unfold in bite-sized chunks.* Give them enough to keep them occupied but not enough to put them off. Far better to lend only one or two learning aids; they can always come back for more

- Make those first Get-Active phone calls as soon as possible. I would suggest that they are made immediately after the Strategy Meeting. The sooner the first Two-to-Ones are booked, the sooner they will sign up their first distributors.

Second, people Going Off-Track at the start causes drop outs

If people start On-Track, you have a chance of keeping them there. If they start Off-Track, it is very difficult to get them back On-Track because the bad habits and wrong conceptions are already becoming ingrained. So first,

Get the Theory of Duplication on your side

The harder you make it for other people to copy what you do, the fewer the people who can follow you. The easiest way to teach them is to make the S.T.A.R. Leadership Programme an essential part of their tuition, and explain to them the importance of duplicating this once their business starts to build. In the process, you will create what few groups manage but which every top distributor I have ever met would dearly love: a standardised tuition system throughout your business.

Get them into the learning habit straight away

For their syllabus, introduce your people to the Training LLAWR as soon as they sign up (Chapter 7, *Get Off To A Winning Start*).

Part of this is to explain that *they are on a six months' apprenticeship*. During that six months, they must not be too concerned about their results. The important thing is to use that time to create a solid grounding for their business, for their attitudes and for their knowledge and understanding of the business. Ask them: *Is it worth this to achieve what they want from the business? Is it worth this to create the lifestyle they want for themselves? In what other business does it take only six months to learn how to earn enough to retire in a few short years?*

Many leaders say to me that this is all very well but they cannot get their people to read! Yes, this is a problem but there is a way round it. When people ask for advice, point them to a relevant chapter or page in a book, ask them to read it and then get back to you if that doesn't solve the problem. With those who will do it (not all will, but they are not going to last anyway), it will very much streamline and accelerate their learning and take a lot of work off your hands, allowing you to get on with other things. It is also *very* duplicatable.

Of course some people will have genuine problems with literacy. The message you must give them is clear: if they want to be as good as they can be, reading is essential. Tapes and videos are not substitutes for reading (see Chapter 7, *Get Off To A Winning Start*). I have found, time and again, distributors with reading problems whose abilities have improved dramatically because they took my advice and trained themselves to develop a reading habit, starting with just a few pages a day. If even this is impossible for them, help them to find professional advice. For distributors with enough Drive, the enormous benefits of learning to read network marketing and personal development books may be just the motivation they need to improve their literacy!

If you use this approach with reluctant readers, they will find that much the quickest and easiest way to teach their people, too, will be to refer them to written texts—and then they will become converts to reading!

There is a hidden and very important point here:

Don't base your decisions on what non-achievers *won't* do, base them on what achievers *need* to do, then encourage the non-achievers to follow suit

---

... because your achievers will read anything they can get their hands on if you show them how it might accelerate them on their path to success and help their people to do better.

Finally, also as part of the Training LLAWR, encourage your people to build their own library of training materials—the more the better—and to develop the *Thirty-Minutes-A-Day Habit.*

Stress the importance of a Hunger to Learn

A Hunger to Learn is one of the *Six Winning Attitudes*. But the little food of thirty minutes a day study will not satisfy a genuine Hunger to Learn. Help people to see that the only way to satisfy the craving of a *real* Hunger to Learn is to realise that

---

Every situation is a learning situation, if they will only let it be so

---

Remember that, according to the Theory of Duplication, if *you* start new distributors in this way, so will they.

Third, failing to create momentum in their group makes people drop out

People who fail to get early results are much more likely to drop out. But don't assume that, because a group has good early results, it has generated ongoing momentum: sometimes the early results fizzle out.

A group with ongoing momentum is one which has one or more anchored legs. What this means, and how to anchor a leg, is explained on page 210.

Because the company you have joined has momentum going does not mean that you will get momentum going in your own group. Equally, because you have generated momentum in your group does not mean that any individual distributor downline of you will get momentum going in their business.

Until a distributor gets group momentum going, they are always at risk of dropping out. Once they have momentum going, they are extremely unlikely to drop out. The only answer is for you to recognise this and to make sure that new distributors are always Worked With intensively (provided that they are Staying On-Track) until they have got momentum going, even if this takes several months.

Finally, too much time to think makes people drop out

If people have too much time to think, real or imaginary doubts can grow and fester at frightening speed. Work on the principle that, if they have things to do, they will not have time to worry.

Any actions you take to fast-track them—including the fast sponsoring techniques in Chapter 14 of *Breakthrough Sponsoring & Retailing*—will automatically help to overcome this problem. But, for the most advanced and exciting fast-track technique in the industry, just read on!

Chapter 14

The All-Out Massive Action Programme—The Fast Way To Build A Solid Business

Now hold onto your hats! Here, for the first time in print, is the *All-Out Massive Action Programme*, the most exciting and by far the fastest *solid* way to build a business.

The real purpose of this plan is to overcome the first of the leaders' and teachers' 'Pigs': *Getting people to make Get-Active phone calls*!

It is the most exciting because massive, concentrated effort is being applied to everyone's Contact List as soon as they sign up. It is the most exciting because people see results in days rather than weeks, or weeks rather than months. It is the most exciting because everyone Works With each other in partnership, no one works on their own, and that is much more motivating than people struggling on in isolation.

It is the fastest way to build a business because it telescopes work—a programme that would take most distributors weeks or months is concentrated into a few days. And it is by far the fastest way to generate *momentum* in your group. Groups only really start to rocket ahead when they achieve momentum.

It is the most solid way to build a business because everyone is spending all their time Working With and getting far better training than they normally would. Working With dramatically cuts drop-out rates among those distributors who agree to use it.

It is the most solid way to build a business because it is by far the best way to overcome people's worries about whether they are 'good' enough to do the job. Even the least charismatic and talented of people will build a strong group more quickly by using this technique, provided they are prepared to 'have a go'.

Despite all its advantages, it is best to warn you in advance that only a small proportion of your people will be prepared to commit the time and effort that the Action Programme demands. But, once two or three set an example of what can be achieved, you will find it increasingly easy to sell the idea to the others!

So how does the All-Out Massive Action Programme work?

The Action Programme brings together three proven principles:

• Phoning their Contact List intensively to arrange Two-to-Ones and generate momentum in the business, *together with…*

• Intensively Working With a manageable number of downlines who will commit themselves to fast-tracking their businesses

• Although this is the quickest and best way to build a business, recognising that only a tiny percentage of new distributors can do these two things on their own.

All big business builders work their Contact Lists intensively. Combine this with the impact of intensive, focused Working With and the results can be spectacular. To fast-track the growth of your own business, here is what you need to do…

Week 1

1. Starting on Monday, because this is psychologically a good day, attack your own Contact List, making 10 to 20 calls a day. The more calls you make, the quicker your

business will take off! Book to see anyone interested as soon as possible.

2. When you have sponsored the first person who **(a)** will give you a Contact List of *at least* 100 names and **(b)** will agree to join the Action Programme and Work With you intensively over the next week, stop your warm market phone calls. Let's call this new distributor, 'Mary'.

   i) You may find Mary on Monday or Tuesday, after just 10 or 20 calls. However, if you are unlucky, you may need all 100 calls to find her. That does not matter because, if you Work With her properly, your business is going to take off anyway, whether you find her sooner or later.

   ii) Many people will not agree to (a) and (b) above, so *please note that you may have to sponsor several people before finding your Mary.*

3. Sit down with Mary and diary in as much time as possible to work together in the following week. It is only for a week so, if Mary is part time, you may have to ask her to sacrifice some of her regular commitments.

4. When you find Mary, don't cancel the rest of your Two-to-One appointments. They have been booked and out of courtesy they must be seen; and you can use them to start Mary's training in Two-to-Ones.

5. If anyone from these appointments wants to join the Action Programme you may have a problem freeing up the time to Work With them intensively, so get them going immediately in the conventional way. Then book them into the first free week you have in your Action Programme. Alternatively, you can **Stack** them under Mary, or another suitable downline. If you are running the Action Programme, I would recommend that you only stack under distributors who agree to run it with you. For general advice on stacking, see Chapter 14 in *Breakthrough Sponsoring & Retailing*.

Week 2

6. On the Monday, start making phone calls with Mary as intensively as possible. Because you must give Mary a good example and are also in a leadership relationship with her, you really should be able to make 20 phone calls a day, especially bearing in mind that Mary will increasingly do more of the calls herself as her confidence increases.

7. Stop further phone calls on Mary's behalf when the two of you have found *two* distributors off Mary's list who agree to (a) and (b) in step 2 above. If you have stacked someone under Mary from *your* Contact List (see step 5 above) you will only have to find one person off her Contact List.

Week 3

8. On the Monday, you take one of Mary's new distributors and Mary takes the other, both of you doing exactly the same as you have just done with Mary.

Week 4 onwards

9. Keep repeating the process, working further down Mary's leg of your business, and making sure everyone else is doing the same.

10. Bring together everyone who is working the Action Programme for regular sizzle sessions (see Chapter 21). With all this action going on, this is the best way to meet and support your most dynamic new people.

11. Don't leave Mary's leg until it is properly anchored (see Chapter 22). But, as each leg gets anchored, start the process again with a new leg.

You will need to be flexible with the timings

Although I have given an example of a three week plan, in practice, there is a lot of luck involved:

1. You cannot always book the Two-to-Ones to be seen that week. Some may hang over to next week or even later

2. Luck dictates how many people on any given Contact List happen to need the business now, and will therefore sign up

3. Not everyone either wants to, or can, start the Action Programme straight away.

But the principle behind the All-Out Massive Action Programme still holds true even if it takes weeks or months longer. Even if you do not find two people for a new distributor in their first week, you will find them very much more quickly using this method than in any other way.

Just note how, by building a commitment to the All-Out Massive Action Programme in your group, you are *automatically* building habits of Urgency in Action and Working With into the culture of your group.

Get the Chicken List included

Remember what we learnt in Appendix II of *Breakthrough Sponsoring & Retailing*: that the Chicken List is by definition the hottest part of anyone's warm market because the people on it are either those best known to the distributor or the people of whom the distributor is most in awe. I have yet to find a distributor who did not have a Chicken List, including me!

You cannot afford to lose the hottest part of people's warm market! So, as soon as you feel confident enough to insist, only Work With people who agree to include their Chicken List in their Contact List.

How to help with the phone call

Both Working With and the All-Out Massive Action Programme are based on the concept that people will make *many times more* phone calls with someone else than on their own.

Before you begin the Action Programme, be sure you have mastered the elements of the simple phone call in Chapter 11, *Get Off To A Winning Start.*

In your first session with Mary, explain the phone call, check for understanding and help her develop her scripts. Then make the first few calls for her, to show her how it is done. If possible, fit a second phone to the socket using a double adaptor, so she can listen to both sides of the call (but she should not join in the conversation—only one person per call is the rule).

As soon as she has the confidence, let her make a few calls and be very encouraging about her efforts; people are very sensitive at this stage. To avoid a situation of Dependency, let Mary make more and more of the phone calls as her confidence increases.

When you are helping with phone calls, it is easier for you if people come to your house, rather than you going to their's. You can also Work With more people because you are not wasting time travelling. Make sure they cover the cost of calls. However, if a distributor does not know you, and your house does not reflect the image of a successful businessperson, go to their's.

Turbocharging the All-Out Massive Action Programme

Although I have given you the example of Working With one person a week on the Action Programme, if you are full-time you can actually Work With two or even three people a week—although the latter needs stamina and careful planning. Even if you don't think you could sustain this long-term, you can set yourself a short-term target of taking on three people a week for, say your first six weeks. I think you can see the explosive effect this will have on your business.

A good way to turbocharge the phone call part of the Action Programme is to get access to two phone lines. If you can afford it, you could have a second line installed at your home—you can also use it for a fax machine. Given that most distributors should be able to make their own calls after an hour or two of coaching, with two lines you can:

- Make calls on their behalf on one line, while they make calls on the other, *or*
- Coach an inexperienced distributor on one line while a more experienced person uses the other line, *or*
- Have two distributors making calls, while you alternate between them, giving them feedback and taking some calls for each in turn to give them a break.

Once you build up experience with this approach, you can even work with a third line and three distributors. Imagine the excitement and momentum that this could generate in your business!

Part-timers

The full-blooded Action Programme only works with full-timers or with part-timers who will commit every evening plus weekends for a few weeks to get their business started.

An alternative with part-timers is to look for five distributors then spend a specific day or evening a week with each—Mondays with the first, Tuesdays with the second, and so on. Adapt this according to circumstances: you may find one distributor who can give you two or even three days or evenings a week. You won't generate the same massive group momentum, but you may have no option and part-timers who agree to (a) and (b) deserve the same support.

What should you do about people who refuse (a) or (b)?

Many distributors write off people who will not do a proper Contact List or who will not Work With them to phone their people. But, if you keep in touch in the right way, some will join the All-Out Massive Action Programme later with the added bonus that they have found out the hard way how *not* to do it! In the meantime:

1. Try to get them to commit to a BACTA and phone them daily as outlined on page 145

2. If you cannot get a BACTA, phone twice a week just to ask how they are getting on: I recommend Wednesday, because it is nicely mid-week, and Friday, because it is seen as the end of the week.

Remember, don't put any pressure on them—just ask them if there is any way in which you can help. If they are finding the going difficult (and they usually are!), an offer from you to make some phone calls with them 'just to see what the problem is' or 'just to get things going' might be accepted with a sigh of relief! Keep contacting them regularly until they either convert to the All-Out Massive Action Programme or become inactive.

An alternative approach for experienced distributors

If, by the time you read this, you have been working for a while as a distributor, you may not have a big enough Contact List left to work this system. So pull your leaders together and train them to bring new distributors in on the All-Out Massive Action Programme. Then Work With each of your leader's legs in turn, helping them to get the Action Programme going in each one.

The All-Out Massive Action Programme makes sponsoring easier!

All the activity generated by the Action Programme creates excitement and momentum in your business, and this makes sponsoring easier for everyone.

How much more powerful is it when you
can say to a contact: 'Look at the business I
have just built with one of my people.
Would you like me to do the same for you?'

Bear in mind that it is not just you who can make this
statement, *but increasing numbers of distributors in your group
who have taken up the All-Out Massive Action Programme for
themselves.*

But, even if a new distributor fast-tracks their business with
the Action Programme, the initial excitement may not be
sustained. The first flush of their enthusiasm coupled with
your own Urgency in Action will get most people through
their early days, but longer lasting results will demand
more sustained determination. So, in the next chapter, I
will show you how to teach your people to develop the
Bulldozer Mentality they need to keep them going until
they finally achieve their goals.

Chapter 15

Teaching A Bulldozer Mentality

Drive is the most important of the Six Winning Attitudes. A Bulldozer Mentality creates Drive. It is its motivating force, whereas Urgency in Action is how you express your Drive from day-to-day.

The best antidote to dropping out is a Bulldozer Mentality. You need to get the message across to new distributors that, if they keep going for long enough, they simply must succeed! You also need to get across just how important a Bulldozer Mentality is: *that no amount of knowledge, talent or support will ever make up for not having a Bulldozer Mentality.*

A Bulldozer Mentality is not a talent, as many people seem to think. It is a habit which anyone can acquire.

A Bulldozer Mentality is a habitual way to react to difficult circumstances in a positive, determined, 'unstoppable' way

---

It is a compensation mechanism given to us by God or Nature to overcome obstacles. People who have a Bulldozer Mentality often acquired it early in life because they *had* to, to compete successfully against those with more natural ability.

Because it is normally developed as a response to problems, talented people are less likely to develop such a strong Bulldozer Mentality; as their advantages allow them to coast through their early years with less effort. This is why people who have both a Bulldozer Mentality and a lot of talent are rare, fortunately for us lesser mortals! When they get out into the wide world only to find that talent by itself is not enough to get them to the top, it is quite common to find that they will not Work With you to develop the habit.

One reason why some people do not develop a Bulldozer Mentality later in life is because they do not realise they *can* do so, because they think it is a talent, not a habit which can be learnt. However, even if you show them the way, the majority will still find it too hard to change their habits of action and reaction. But, if you can help just one downline in a hundred to develop a Bulldozer Mentality and teach your people to do the same, the Geometric Progression will ensure that the impact on your business will be very substantial indeed!

In this chapter, I will show you nine proven ways to help people to develop determination and thereby increase their Drive.

1. Enjoyment develops a Bulldozer Mentality

Enjoyment is the 'E' of being an ACTTER and its role in determination is another reason why it is so important (see Chapter 4, *Breakthrough Sponsoring & Retailing*).

If a person *enjoys* doing something enough,
how much determination will they need?

The more someone enjoys doing something, the less determination they need to do it. So the more you can create an exciting, enjoyable atmosphere in your group the less you and your distributors will need to rely on grim determination.

2. Pride (one of the Six Winning Attitudes) develops a Bulldozer Mentality

Great Pride leads to Belief + Passion, which = Conviction, and this is essential to the long-term success of all distributors. It is their best defence against doubts, set-backs, uninformed media coverage, or failed distributors who attack network marketing or try to shift the blame for their own failures onto their sponsors.

Pride has been discussed in depth in both the earlier titles in the S.T.A.R. Leadership Programme.

If a distributor really *believes* with *passion* in what they are doing, how much of a Bulldozer Mentality will they need?

---

3. Crystal clear burning ambitions develop a Bulldozer Mentality

You will have much more success as a teacher if you believe that helping distributors to achieve what they want through network marketing is much more important than showing them how to succeed as distributors. Showing people what to do is easy; *motivating* them to do it is the problem and this is where personal goals can help.

If a distributor wants something badly enough, won't that give them the Bulldozer Mentality to keep going?

Used correctly, personal goal-setting is the most massively powerful tool that you, as a winning leader and teacher, can call on to build your business. If you could help *all* the distributors in your business to find the goals which *really* turned them on, would you need to work at motivating them, *or would you just point them in the right direction and watch them go?* If all your downlines had goals which *really* excited them, *would, or would not, your business explode?*

The subject of goals is dealt with throughout the S.T.A.R. Leadership Programme, including the companion books *Supercharge Yourself!* and *Target Success!*, because the whole reason for joining the business is to achieve goals in life. And the way you succeed in achieving your goals is by

Focusing On Your Goals, and then, by *Focusing Your Actions On Success*.

Your biggest problem is to persuade people how important crystal clear, hungrily desired goals are to their success, so I'll show you how to deal with a couple of typical reactions:

'Goal-setting is very "American", a bit "over the top" or "hypy" and not the "British" way of doing things'

Let me make a categorical statement which you can use with sceptics:

No matter how well someone has done up to now, they would have got further faster, and dealt with more obstacles more easily *and with more enthusiasm*, if they had used *effective* goal-setting

---

'I am very self-motivated. Setting goals is not going to motivate me to work any harder!'

These are the people you really want in your business. The more self-motivated people you have, the better your business will be, but *only* if you can get them to focus! The trouble is that many of them chase their tails like Catherine wheels instead of shooting off like a rocket aimed unerringly at their goals.

They misunderstand the purpose of goals. For people like this, goals are not to *motivate*, they are to *focus* actions on purposes, to change them from Catherine wheels, which only chase their tails, to rockets aimed unerringly at their targets. So explain to them that, no matter how self-motivated and successful people are, if their aim is to be the best they can be, they will go further faster, and overcome a greater number of obstacles more effectively and with greater enthusiasm, with goals than without them.

You may find that the following diagram, **The Goal-to-Goal Ladder,** helps to get across the message to people about the importance of goals:

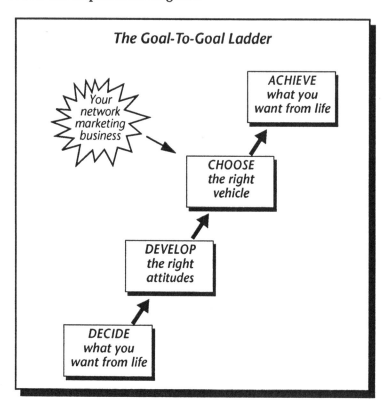

This is what people do not understand:

Goals (which are what you want from life) both *start* and *finish* the process of achieving your aims

---

The process you carry out in every action you take in life is:

1. Decide what you want to achieve

2. Develop the attitude to achieve it

3. Choose the vehicle—in other words, how you are going to achieve it

4. Achieve what you set out to achieve.

This is how we carry out every task we do, even the simplest everyday ones. Try to make a cup of coffee without following those steps and see how far you get! Yet in work, although it is the most time-consuming activity for most, people hardly ever use their occupation as a vehicle for getting what they want from life.

> **People are taught to focus on the job,**
> **which is what their employer wants them**
> **to do, not on what the job will do for them**

You can now see clearly why some self-motivated people never seem to achieve what they should: they have got the two middle bits of the Goal-to-Goal Ladder *very* right but it is the two ends which are missing. The result is that they squander their time on tasks which lead nowhere.

> **They are focusing on the tasks in hand, not**
> **on what those tasks will do for them. If**
> **they were to focus on their goals, they**
> **would do only those tasks which**
> **contributed directly to them and reject the**
> **rest**

Most jobs barely sustain people in a particular lifestyle which is why someone coined the phrase: **J-O-B = Just Over Broke!** That is all that most people ever achieve.

Now, in network marketing, they have the opportunity to do more—to get what they want from life, so let's just decide what that is ... *yourself included, if you have not already done it!* Some teachers and leaders ask distributors to practise goal-setting even though they do not practise it themselves. This is a clear case of trying to side-step the Theory of Duplication which states, *People tend to copy what you do, not do what you say.* As I said before, *Practise what you preach!*

If you ask people what their aims and ambitions are, they will usually reply within the restrictions of what they believe they could *actually* afford or *realistically* achieve. This may not be what they would *really*, deep-down, like to accomplish. But what, they think, is the point of telling you some deep-down secret desire when they know they will never in a million years be able to achieve it? So what they tell you may be a compromise desire—in other words, something they think is within the limit of their attainment and, at the same time, something they think you will not find laughable or unrealistic. The trouble is:

A compromise desire is almost never hot enough to truly motivate a person to achieve it

---

Therefore, you may have to remove any barriers which your distributors have created in their own minds against daring to admit, perhaps even to themselves, what they would really like to achieve. The way to do this is to:

1. Create *trust* between you. If you are an ACTTER, you will already have achieved this

2. Make sure they understand the importance of personal goals to their success but that these must be goals which they find truly exciting

3. Create a framework within which they can really let their imaginations run riot. This will happen if you can remove the limitations your distributors have put on their own minds about what is possible and what is impossible.

The actual techniques for goal-setting are in Chapter 3 of *Get Off To A Winning Start*, and you will find a convenient form for the exercise in *Target Success!* Also, because goals are such an important part of personal development, you really need to see *Supercharge Yourself!* or a similar book on self-development.

4. Clear satisfactions from work develop the Bulldozer Mentality

Many occupations can be carried out well enough even though the person hates what they are doing. This is not so with network marketing: no-one can be an even adequate distributor unless they get some clear satisfactions from doing the job. It will reinforce your distributor's Bulldozer Mentality if you help them to isolate what satisfactions they get and ask them to contemplate them for only a few minutes a day. What does satisfaction at work mean to people? Everyone is different, but here are some ideas:

• In some people it means enjoyment of what they do

• In others, pride in themselves for a job well done

• Others seek the respect of family, friends, customers, people who work for them, bosses, competitors or the industry for being good at what they do

• In others, it means creating or maintaining the lifestyle they want for themselves or their family

• In others, it means helping people (customers, downlines) through what they do

• In others, it is a sense of mission, a sense of destiny or a crusading zeal for what they can achieve through what they do.

As you can see, this is quite different from seeking goals and, unlike goals which you have to distil down to very few, the more satisfactions a distributor can find the better.

The more satisfactions a distributor can find for doing what they do, the more motivated they will be to do it

---

5. Getting quick, early results develops a Bulldozer Mentality

We have already covered this in Chapter 13.

6. Treating this business with the seriousness it deserves develops a Bulldozer Mentality

Being a distributor has perhaps the lowest entry requirement of any potentially high-level business or career, which means that you need no qualifications or experience, little talent, only a minimal investment, no selection procedure to pass, and that entry is easy and immediate.

One of the penalties of the low entry requirement is that it actually helps people to fail because they do not take the business seriously enough.

Many other businesses require a lot of time, red tape and effort just to get to the starting gate; going to all that trouble in itself creates a determination to make the business succeed. If you want a job, just getting through the selection procedure can be extremely tough. But, with network marketing, starting up is all too easy and this can generate a feeling of *Easy come, easy go.*

To show you how the ease of entry can lead to an unintentional loss of Drive, let me ask you a question:

'If you had invested £50,000 in your network marketing business and put your house on the line, and had just spent six months' hard work wrestling with bank managers, lawyers, estate agents, local government 'officiousals' and

'uncivil' servants, recruiting and managing staff, briefing printers, negotiating with suppliers and dealing with utility companies just to get started, would you be working harder right now?'

The only people I have ever found to honestly answer 'No' to this question are those who did eventually succeed. *They succeeded because they **did** take the business as seriously as they could, right from the start.*

Now, if you are reading this, the chances are that you are a motivated person who has come into network marketing with every intention of doing whatever it takes to succeed and you probably believed, up to now, that you were putting in all the effort you could, even if you are part-time. If a determined person like yourself would actually have worked harder if *you* had invested all that money and effort, *what effect do you think the low cost and ease of entry are having on the levels of determination and commitment of other, perhaps less ambitious, people in your group?*

But, before I show you how to tackle this problem, here is another side of the same coin...

7. Showing people that the rewards justify a little Patience develops a Bulldozer Mentality

People often drop out due to impatience. They want results yesterday and, when these do not come, they drop out. Yet many people look to network marketing as the answer to some serious problems in their lives and for that it deserves great respect—respect which they are not giving, because it has been too easy to start the business.

A good question to ask at trainings is whether anyone there has started a new business that involved borrowing money and putting their houses on the line. There almost always is. Then ask how long they were prepared to wait before they broke even or got into profit. A typical answer is two or three years.

People who borrow money and put their houses at risk will wait for over two years to see results; yet network market-eers who borrow no money, do not have to put up their houses as security *and* have far more to go for, give up after days, weeks or months! If such a big reward is on offer, isn't it worth exercising a bit of patience?

To deal with this problem and the previous one of not tak-ing the business seriously enough, get your distributors to change their conception of the business. Instead of measur-ing the business by what it cost, get them to quantify it in terms of *what they can get out of it.* For instance:

Network marketing is perhaps the one way for the distributor to solve their ATAC Equation:

Abundant

Time,

Abundant

Cash

... **A**bundant **T**ime to do the things they want to do;
... **A**bundant **C**ash to do them with.

Explain to them that their ATAC Equation can be solved only by ATTACKing the things which get in the way of it. Show them how to value their business, not by what it costs to join and run, but by the goals they can achieve through it—in other words, solving their ATAC Equation.

Ambitious people are motivated by money, by status or by both

We are all motivated by the wish to earn the money we need to lead the lifestyle we want. Get your distributors to place that value on their business. For instance, if a distrib-utor needs to earn £30,000 a year to sustain their lifestyle, theirs is a £30,000 business

Some distributors are motivated also by *status.* They can measure this in one of two ways: by their corporate position in the network, or by the number of people 'employed' (i.e., distributors) in their business.

For those who see status in terms of their corporate position, keep reminding them that they can reach the top position in the network within one to five years from starting. But ask how long, if ever, would it take them to reach the status of a top position in any other career open to them?

If what motivates them is the kudos of being able to say that they have, for example, 500 or 5,000 distributors in their group, focus them on the fact that this is the value they should place on their business.

Of course, some distributors may be motivated by more than one of these attractions. The important thing is to find out what will excite them about the business or the goals they can achieve through it, then educate them to value the business in these terms. They must get rid of, once and for all, the *Easy come, easy go* attitude which stops them from taking network marketing seriously enough.

8. Treating the business as their last chance develops a Bulldozer Mentality

> How much more determination would people put into making a success of their business if they really believed this was their last chance?

This is turning the situation into a 'must' and,

> When people see an action as a 'must', they will do it. If they see a desired result as a 'must', they will go for it

In many cases, it may not be too far from the truth to say that this is the last *realistic* chance for a distributor: for redundant executives whose only crime is that they are over 40, for bankrupt businesspeople who can no longer get credit or finance, for women returning to work after 20 years of parenting, and for anyone who has no other realistic way of creating the income they need.

Even for the most committed people, the comfort of knowing that they have other options will take at least some of the edge off their focus and performance. So you will do your people a favour if you can get them to behave as if they really do have nowhere else to go if this business does not succeed for them.

Put cards up in your bedroom, on your bathroom mirror, on the sun visor of your car and inside the lid of your briefcase, saying, '**THIS IS MY LAST CHANCE!!**' British people in particular feel self-conscious about using cards but, if they see you using them, some of them might do the same.

9. Warning your distributors of 'The Pigs Around The Corner' develops a Bulldozer Mentality

'The Pigs Around The Corner' were covered in detail in Chapter 5 of *Get Off To A Winning Start*.

10. Taking the responsibilities of teaching and leading seriously develops a Bulldozer Mentality

Many people find it difficult to motivate themselves. But put a *responsible* person into a training and leadership role and they will find reserves of determination and toughness they never knew they had. Point out to such people that they will make or break other people by their own example, and they will rise to the challenge. Don't be frightened to do this—people who do not rise to the occasion will not survive anyway.

There is only one purpose in life for a Bulldozer Mentality: to help people to overcome problems... problems... problems... Let's look at ways to deal with these in the next chapter.

Chapter 16

Problems... Problems... Problems...
—And How To Overcome Them!

This chapter is extremely important to you because the only reason your distributors will drop out is because of problems—unless, of course, network marketing is simply the wrong occupation for them to be involved in. Some of these problems are entirely self-inflicted—like the refusal to learn or to apply what they have learnt. Others are barriers imposed by circumstances which distributors come across as they build their business.

As we discussed in the last chapter, the value of a Bulldozer Mentality is only in overcoming problems, but the *knowledge* of how to overcome problems is equally important, something this chapter will give you. Although I address these ideas to you, you should pass these same ideas to your people.

Almost every problem encountered in network marketing will have already been dealt with successfully by literally hundreds of thousands, if not millions, of distributors the world over. There are only a tiny number of problems which cannot be overcome successfully by almost every distributor if they go about it in the right way.

So, although most people see a problem as the *cause* of failure, it is not. Given that the great majority of distributors have the ability to overcome it, it follows that:

Failure is not caused by a problem. It is caused by insufficient personal motivation to overcome the problem

---

Problems are lessons in disguise

Unquestionably, adversity is the best teacher. The overwhelming reason why people improve is because they *have* to, to overcome a problem, or *want* to, to prepare themselves for the greater problems which will stand in the way of greater achievement. If people got what they wanted when they wanted, without the need to improve, most people would never develop themselves. Seen in this way:

Problems are opportunities for self-improvement

Met in the right way, life's difficulties and troubles will not arrest our progress but will actually speed us to our goals because they spur us to call into play new forces and powers to overcome them—forces and powers which we can then use to help us on the rest of our journey.

But this approach will only work if we see problems as learning opportunities. It could be said that problems are sent to us specifically so that we can learn the lessons from them. If we do not see problems in this way, the whole pain and heartache they cause us is wasted. So,

---

Whenever a problem occurs, ask: 'What is it trying to teach me?'

Forewarned is forearmed

The impact of a problem is greatly magnified if it is unexpected. Indeed, the unexpectedness of a problem can be very much worse than the problem itself. Good sailors do not fear rough seas or high winds; it is the more modest wave or gust of wind catching them unawares which is the real danger.

This means that you need a much greater degree of personal motivation or a stronger Bulldozer Mentality to overcome an unexpected problem than to deal with an expected one. Therefore, it is an important part of your job as a teacher to tell your distributors what problems to expect and to give them strategies to deal with them when they occur. This is why we isolate the problems consistently faced by every distributor as 'Pigs Around The Corner' (the 'Pigs' for leaders and teachers are covered in Chapter 5).

The 'Nos': fear of rejection

The fear of rejection is one of the hardest problems a distributor has to deal with so, although I gave you strategies to deal with them earlier in the Programme, I will summarise them for you here.

'Nos' go with the territory

Every distributor is going to get a lot of 'Nos' for each 'Yes'.

Successful distributors are simply those who accept more 'Nos' than unsuccessful ones

---

Get back to focusing on your purposes, not on your actions

With so much to go for, it isn't worth putting up with a few 'Nos'?

Don't take 'Nos' personally

If you really felt that a contact could have benefited by signing up, that contact was not saying 'No' to you, but to their own hopes and aspirations.

We are in the sorting business

Your first job is to sort the wheat from the chaff, those who might be interested in the opportunity or the product from those who are not.

Therefore,

> **All we want are decisions from your
> contacts and it does not matter whether
> those decisions are 'Yes' or 'No'**

This is a numbers game; if you approach enough people, enough people *will* say 'Yes'.

Show that every 'No' has a value

You need an example of the value of a 'No'. For example, let's say that you are selling a product on which you make £50 profit per sale. Say that your conversion rate is 10%, which means that, for every ten potential customers you see, you average one sale. As you have to unlock nine 'No' doors to reach the one marked 'Yes', each 'No' is worth £5 to you.

I once explained this to a direct salesman. 'Good heavens!' he said. 'If I knock on every door in Birmingham, I'll make a fortune!' I hadn't quite thought of it in that way but had to agree that the theory was sound.

He set out to do that and, every time a prospect said 'No', he replied, 'Thank you for your kind attention—and thank you for the £5 you have just earned me!' Not only did he find that this overcame his reluctance to door-knock, but he actually made a lot of extra sales from curious house-holders who said, 'Just a minute! How have I just earned you £5?' Once they started talking, a sale could follow, or, if not a sale, a referral.

And, yes, he did make a lot of money because he no longer took 'Nos' personally and therefore found it easy to knock doors all day.

Now, I am sure that you will agree that prospecting in network marketing is very much less daunting than knocking doors, so if this technique worked for the salesman, it can surely work for you and your people!

To overcome problems, get them into perspective

A problem, when it first arises, can seem to be overwhelming. But you can make it seem to be much more manageable just by changing your perspective on it. Here are some ways in which you can do that.

First, does the problem even exist?

Or is it only in your mind? Are you anticipating a problem which may never happen?

A famous businessman once asked me, 'Can *you* remember the problems you had this time last week?' Some—yes, I could remember easily. *But I had great difficulty in recalling the bulk of them.* He then went on to say, 'If you file all your problems in the waste-paper basket now, by this time next week, most of them will have either cured themselves or disappeared.' In other words, they either do not exist or they have been inflamed out of all proportion.

Have you any other options for getting the income required?

If the answer is 'No', this realisation may be enough to help you find the resolve necessary to overcome the problem. Of course, if you have other options, they should be explored so that you stop 'sitting on the fence' and go whole-heartedly for one option or the other. Even on a part-time basis, network marketing does not take kindly to half-hearted measures, so you must make up your mind: commit totally either to this business or to your other option.

Problems are part of the business and can be overcome!

Successful people have already had to overcome them, otherwise they would not be successful. Successful people meet much the same obstacles as unsuccessful ones; the *only* difference between the two is that *successful people are prepared to overcome more obstacles.* This is because successful people understand the nature of obstacles much more clearly than other people do.

Successful people realise that, in order to achieve any goal, they will have to negotiate a set number of obstacles; the only trouble is that no-one knows how many (see page 62) What if someone gives up just when the next obstacle would have been the last? Successful people are not prepared to take that risk, unsuccessful people are.

'Is my goal worth the effort required to overcome this obstacle?'

The difference between success and failure is often nothing more than that one person can see quite clearly what success in overcoming that obstacle will bring, another cannot.

So ask yourself, *'Is my goal worth the effort required to overcome this obstacle?'* each time you meet a problem; in other words, *Focus on your purposes* (part of the Winning Attitudes). It is amazing how often people, who were about to give in, suddenly find hidden reserves when they do this!

If you look at the problems you have successfully overcome, you will see that they are no longer the looming obstacles they appeared to be at the time. With the benefit of hindsight, you can see that:

A problem is not a barrier: it is only a temporary diversion on the road to success

---

Learning from hindsight makes it easier, when you meet future problems, to decide that your goal is only a temporary diversion and therefore worth the effort required to overcome the problem.

If you know with absolute certainty that you can overcome a problem, is it a problem any longer?

There is no such thing as achieving any success without having to overcome some obstacles. The point about obstacles is not that they exist but how important they are in your mind. If a person can see a way *they feel comfortable with* to overcome an obstacle, they will do so and continue on their path towards success; if they cannot see a solution *acceptable to themselves*, they will give up their search for success and drop out.

So often, overcoming a problem is only having the *confidence* that you can do it, plus the *knowledge* of how to overcome it. If you are not sure you can overcome it, each obstacle is built up to be bigger than it actually is; you are seeing the obstacle as it was *before* you tackled it. Successful people, because they are totally confident they will overcome a problem (it is only a question of how), see it as smaller than it actually is; they are seeing it as if *after* it was overcome.

Part of your job as a teacher and leader is to help distributors to develop the confidence to overcome problems along the way, so that it is no longer a case of *if* a problem will be overcome but *how* and *when*. Seen in this way, you are helping them to reduce each problem to the point where they no longer see it as a barrier, but clearly as a temporary diversion.

Make the problem a common one, not one peculiar to them

Help people to understand that the problem is a common one which is quite normal to other distributors, because it then becomes less of a threat. Problems which are seen by people as peculiar to themselves are usually the more dangerous to deal with.

Develop a Bulldozer Mentality in your people

As I said earlier, the purpose of a Bulldozer Mentality is to drive people to success by helping them to overcome problems. The more you can help your distributors to develop that ability (as we discussed in the previous chapter), the more you will reduce their problems to temporary diversions and the less likely they will be to drop out.

Avoid comments like 'When the going gets tough, the tough get going'

Comments like this may sound clever but they are not helpful. You might easily provoke the reaction: 'I don't think I'm tough enough, so I'd better get going!' They certainly do not make someone attempting to deal with a problem feel any better. Comments like this make problems seem more significant than they really are, when your job is to make them *less* significant and therefore easier to deal with.

Plan the route

Finally, if people know exactly where they are going and exactly what they have to do to get there, problems take on a less threatening aspect because they become part of the route—deviations rather than barriers. This involves planning, so let's have a look at that next.

Chapter 17

People Who Fail To Plan, Plan To Fail

Success comes, not from action, but from *focused* or *directed* action

---

... and the quickest and easiest way to *Focus Your Actions On Your Purpose* (part of the Six Winning Attitudes) is to plan your work to achieve it.

The subject of planning your business is covered in depth in *Target Success!*, together with copies of all the relevant planning forms a distributor needs for the whole of their first year. In this chapter, I will cover what is absolutely essential.

I also said in Chapter 11 that I would show you a more sophisticated way of judging who to Work With. The method is to choose those distributors who agree to the Six Planning Commitments I will show you in a moment.

A Catherine wheel looks and sounds terrific as it *whooshes*, spins and showers sparks in all directions, but it is going nowhere! Despite all its power, it can never hit its target so all its actions are in vain. Just like the Catherine wheel, any action which does not contribute directly to what you want is *wasted* action.

Emulate instead the rocket, aiming unerringly at its target

How can you teach a distributor to be a rocket rather than a Catherine wheel? Ask for **Six Planning Commitments**:

1. Will they make a commitment to what they want from the business?

2. Will they make a commitment to your teaching strategy?

3. Will they make a commitment to their Business Activity Agreement?

4. Will they make a commitment to Learning?

5. Will they commit to putting what they learn into practice?

6. Will they commit to doing a proper Contact List?

1. Will they make a commitment to what they want from the business?

This is such a flexible business that, until you know exactly where a distributor wants to go, you can't help them plan their actions to get there. Remember the rule, *Do not impose your aspirations on other people.* It is very easy to *assume* that you know what someone wants but, if you do not take the trouble to find out that they want to go from London to Edinburgh, you may unwittingly give them a route to Brighton.

Distributors fall very broadly into four categories:

- Those who want only to retail
- Those who want to retail and business-build on a part-time basis
- Those who start part-time with the intention of going full-time
- Those aspiring to a high-level business.

Every distributor needs to both know exactly what they want to achieve and make the commitment to do what is necessary to achieve it.

People's ambitions change according to their circumstances. For instance, it is common for people to sign up with every intention of making network marketing a little part-time business, but then they get bitten by the bug and—WOW! They take off! So how do you ensure that your teaching is always on the same wavelength as your distributor's evolving needs? Just keep asking them the question:

'What are you looking for from the business?'

This question should be asked often, because it makes your distributors keep their aims in network marketing in harmony with their changing personal circumstances.

For the same reason, this is a question you should keep asking *yourself*.

2. Will they make a commitment to your teaching strategy?

Once you know what a distributor wants from the business, you can pitch your teaching strategy to their ambitions. Clearly, you will not teach someone who only wants to do a bit of retailing in the same way as you would someone who wants to build a high level business.

Part of your teaching strategy will be to show them *How to work smart, as well as hard*; and *planning* their work is what working smart means. Setting off to Brighton when they want to go to Edinburgh may be working hard but it is hardly working smart.

In other words, you are asking your downlines for a commitment to accept your guidance on how they should best use their time. The time they give to network marketing needs to be *quality time*. For example, if they have decided to allocate ten hours a week to the business, they can either waste that ten hours or, with your guidance, they can pack it with value. The way to achieve quality time is to make sure that both the **Content** and the **Attitude** are right.

Packing time with the right content

Teach your people to devote the whole of their allocated time purely and totally to three of the Four Must-do Activities: retailing, sponsoring and teaching. Any learning activities such as the Thirty-Minutes-A-Day Habit must be done in their own time. And, of course, all other activities which do not earn them money should be confined to 'out of hours'.

An important part of your teaching strategy is that all One-to-Ones should be Two-to-Ones. Some distributors, particularly those from a business or sales background, can obstinately refuse to allow another distributor to go with them to see their contacts. If so, you should be equally obstinate. There is no point in spending valuable time with them because, according to the Theory of Duplication, they will teach their people not to hold Two-to-Ones and this is precisely the habit you do *not* want in your business.

The right attitude to the value of time

But the content of what people do is meaningless by itself. What brings it to life, what really packs value into the time they allocate to network marketing is to show them the importance of bringing both a sense of *Urgency in Action* and *Enjoyment* to their work (the 'E' of being an ACTTER).

This is not a business for time-servers who just go through the motions, but you will find that many people have forgotten how to feel any urgency about work. As for enjoyment, that is an emotion some have long since lost! If a person's mind has become conditioned to linking pain to work, due to years of doing a job from which they got no satisfaction, or suffering under bad management, you may have to teach them how to enjoy work again.

3. Will they make a commitment to their Business Activity Agreement?

The Business Activity Agreement or BACTA pulls together all the targets which experience shows that you and your distributors should set yourselves. At any given time, you will be *directly* Working With a small number of people to help them get their businesses established. The BACTA helps you to direct their actions very specifically towards their purposes and can also be their agreement of what they are prepared to do in return for your help.

But the BACTA also fulfils two other functions. If people *write down* what they say they will do, they are much more likely to do it, and, just as important, they are less likely to deviate. It is easy to stray from a path if it cannot be seen. This is a very common problem among workaholics and is the reason why so many do not get the success their efforts deserve: they can deviate easily from the path because they had not written it down.

Again according to the Theory of Duplication, if you do not use the BACTA yourself as a matter of habit, you will find it much more difficult to get your people to use it.

So what are the targets in the BACTA? They are:

• *The Personal and Downline Contacting Targets.* How many people will a distributor phone each day for themselves and, when their business starts to build, for a downline? This is not how many contacts agree to a meeting, simply how many are phoned. Even if a contact refuses a meeting, the call still counts towards the target because we are just sorting the wheat from the chaff, those who want a look from those who do not

• *The Two-to-One Target.* How many people will a distributor see each week for themselves and, when their business starts to build, for their downlines?

• *The Retailing Target.* How much will they sell each week or each month? Remember the rules:

   i) Everyone has to retail

   ii) How much each person retails is up to them

   iii) *But everyone must set* **at least** *a monthly target and stick to it.*

   If the compensation plan of your company specifies a certain retail turnover to qualify for bonuses and royalties, that is the minimum retail target your distributors should set themselves

- *The 30-Minutes-A-Day Habit* which breaks down to fifteen minutes of new study and fifteen minutes of recapping each day
- *The BOM Target* (if your company promotes them). How many BOMs will they attend each week? (The minimum is one)
- *Your Upline Sizzle.* They must attend your sizzles
- *The Downline Sizzle Target.* How many downline sizzles will they attend each week to help out their people?

The Two-to-One, downline sizzle and downline contacting targets do not apply to new distributors: how many Two-to-Ones they book will depend on the success of their initial contacting, so it cannot be planned at this stage. The downline sizzle and downline contacting targets are not relevant until they have downline distributors.

You will find a special form for the BACTA in my book *Target Success!*

I would not recommend formally presenting new distributors with a BACTA. It looks too threatening. Simply get their agreement to each of the five targets which affect new distributors as part of discussion. Only when they are more experienced should you formalise the arrangement with them. When you get to that stage, the best way is to show them your personal BACTA.

Make sure they fully understand three things:

- The targets they set are their own, not yours. It cannot be said too often that you must take great care not to impose your aspirations on your people
- They should constantly update their targets in line with the needs of their business or in response to changing conditions and advise you of these changes—so the BACTA will often need to be changed weekly
- It will pay you handsomely if you agree a regular time each week for discussing their next week's BACTA with

you. The psychologically best days are Fridays to Sundays, in time to start the new week.

In comfort zone or out of comfort zone?

In terms of setting targets, you will have two sorts of distributor:

• Those who want to work outside their comfort zone, *and*

• Those who will not work outside their comfort zone.

Each requires entirely different teaching and leadership: the first group will drop out from frustration if you attempt to hold them back; the second group will drop out if you push them too hard. So take this into account when you are helping them to set targets.

Those who want to work outside their comfort zone will be a small percentage of your total distributors but they are potentially your leaders. They want to set targets as high as possible. You must make sure that, first, those targets are focusing their actions on achieving their purpose in the best possible way and, second, that they have paced themselves to last the marathon distance. If you let them sprint the first few laps and burn out (like Hyperactive Harold, see page 147), you have just lost that rare commodity, a natural hard worker.

Those who will work only within their comfort zone. These will be the great majority of your distributors. Present training systems tend to brand them as 'drop out' material—*'People who are not prepared to pay the price'* is the expression often used. Trainers too often tell people that they must work outside their comfort zone and that, if they do not, they won't make it. Won't make what? Yes, this is true if someone wants to earn a high income, but many are satisfied with less.

Two rules apply to setting *effective* targets: *Don't impose your aspirations on other people* (which the above trainers are breaking) and *Network marketing is a lot of people doing a lit-*

tle bit. So let's show you how to apply both of these rules to setting a Personal Contacting Target. All this is based on a simple premise:

If you expect too much of people who will not work outside their comfort zones, you will get nothing. If you expect a little, you will get something

---

The Personal Contacting Target

Every leader would like their group to sponsor more people.

The reason why not enough sponsoring goes on is because not enough Get-Active phone calls are being made and, until they are, not enough potential distributors will enter the sponsoring process

---

I should stress that these comments are to help you with people who will not work outside their comfort zone. They do not apply to those who *want* to work outside their comfort zone, nor to distributors using the All-Out Massive Action Programme. To see how Get-Active phone calls are dealt with in that Programme, refer to Chapter 14.

Outside of Working With (i.e. making their calls with them), the contacting target is the best way I know to overcome the first of the teachers' and leaders' 'Pigs': *Getting people to make Get-Active phone calls!*

Most teaching on making warm market phone calls (which is the Get-Active Step) consists of trying to get people to make more phone calls than they really want. But this is breaking the rule, *Do not impose your aspirations on other people.* The more you push, the less you will get because you are setting people up for stress and failure rather than pride in achievement.

So do the complete opposite: encourage people to keep the target *down* to a level which you judge there is a good chance they will really achieve. This way, *A lot of people doing a little* bit will give you amazing results.

For example, say you have 100 distributors. Most group leaders would agree that about ten are doing most of the work so your problem is, how can I make the other 90 do *something*, no matter how little? How many calls a day are those 90 doing? We all agree, not many. But would they agree to making one a day? Yes, they'll all agree, but let's say 50 actually do. That will give you 1,500 calls a month. Are they making that number now?

Because of the stress and self-doubt involved, people often become inactive or drop-out as a direct result of setting themselves targets they cannot keep to. Unless you, as a teacher, control the situation, the scenario you face with a new distributor might be something like this: on day one, they make twenty phone calls; seven on day two, five on day three... By the end of the week, they have virtually stopped. Does this sound familiar? Did *you* do something like this? I did!

So let's start that discussion on the Personal Retailing Target again:

'How many calls can you make a day?'

'Oh, I think I can manage twenty' (Or ten. Everyone thinks they can do that, until they try!).

'Mmmm... Shall we make that five calls a day? Let's just start with five until we see how you get on. We can always put it up later. Get into the habit of making five calls a day and your business will grow just fine. Tell you what, I'll give you a ring tomorrow to see how you got on.'

Once they have set a target, decide from their Contact List who will be phoned today.

Tomorrow, phone them:

> *'How did you get on last night?'*

> *'I managed to make three phone calls.'*

Discuss those three and give advice. Then come back to:

> *'What was the problem with the other two?'*

Listen to the reason they give for not making them.

> *'Are you going back to five calls tonight? Or, be honest, are you a little uncomfortable with making five?'*

> *'Well... yes. To be honest, three was enough!'*

> *'No Problem! Shall we drop your target for a while and see how you get on? Are you comfortable with three, or would two suit you better?'*

> *'No, no. Three was OK. I can do that.'*

They will have two contacts left over from last night, so agree with them the third name for tonight.

The next secret is to follow up contacting targets *every day* with each of the new people you are directly looking after, except, of course, any you made phone calls with on the previous evening. That way, you can harness the power of Constant Repetition. Not only are you creating a habit—and people will *not* develop the contacting habit unless you follow up every day—but you are also, according to the Theory of Duplication, teaching them to teach their people in the same way.

This daily contact also means that you will nip problems in the bud and, if they do not stick to their agreement, you know very quickly whether this person is worth Working With, or whether you need to move onto Working With someone else or sponsoring a new distributor.

Of course, don't miss the opportunity of suggesting to a distributor that they increase their contacting target, if they feel comfortable with doing so in the light of their increasing confidence or motivation.

If a distributor will not agree to a BACTA, use a different strategy as shown on page 111.

The Retailing Target

With regard to the retailing target, the number of people they will have to show the product to, to hit that target, is going to depend on how good they are at retailing.

Retailing abilities vary enormously from one distributor to another, from those who can retail to almost anyone to those who can retail to almost no-one. It may be that someone used to dealing with the general public in this way (a salesperson, a teacher, a receptionist and so on) may only have to show the product to two people to get a sale, whereas people who are not used to dealing with the general public (housewives who have been out of the job-market for years to bring up their children, manual workers or craftspeople, office-bound people from clerks to directors, or many professional people) may have to show the product to twenty people. That does not matter. If they both need to make two sales a week, the first person needs only to see four people; the other will need to see forty. But, if that is what they must do, they must do it.

The key to achieving targets is Consistency

There are other really effective, business-building ways to plan and target work. For these, see *Target Success!* But setting proper targets is only half the battle; if you want to help your people to achieve them, you should also explain the importance and the meaning of **Consistency**. In other words, they must carry out each of the Must-Do activities *consistently* every day, every week or every month depending on the requirements of each target.

You may have noticed that distributors are not asked to set themselves a target for the number of hours they are prepared to devote each week to building their businesses. This is not an essential target because the number of hours worked is less important than what is done in those hours.

All the targets in the BACTA relate to *productivity* because it is productivity that you want. However, there is no reason why you cannot add that target if you so wish, either as a general rule or in cases where you think it might be relevant.

Watch out for Hyperactive Harold!

Hyperactive Harold tells you he will put in ten hours a week, and then puts in ten hours a day. He goes off like a rocket, lighting up the sky with a shower of sparks. He forgets to take his mother-in-law to Bingo, his wife only sees him when he needs a clean shirt, his children ask, 'Mummy, mummy—who's that strange man?' and his boss gets angry at the amount of unfinished work on Hyperactive Harold's desk.

But you think, 'Great! Hyperactive Harold is really taking off! He's going to be a real benefit to my business!'

Except for one thing: six weeks later, Hyperactive Harold falls out of your business. His mother-in-law has hit him with a rolling pin, his wife has threatened divorce, he suddenly realises how much he is missing his children and his boss has sent him a warning letter.

Hyperactive Harold's sponsor did himself no favours by not advising him to hold back and stick to his BACTA!

4. Will they make a commitment to Learning?

A Hunger to Learn is one of the Six Winning Attitudes. The easiest way to show new distributors the learning routes open to them is to take them through the **Training LLAWR** (Chapter 7, *Get Off To A Winning Start*).

In addition, point out that, if they are going to bring warm market contacts (i.e., people they know) into their business, don't they *owe* it to their contacts to *learn* as much as they can so that they can *teach* them as well as they can?

5. Will they commit to putting what they learn into practice?

Of course, learning only comes to life when it is put into action. The best way to ensure that you and your people consistently put your learning into action is to plan.

Plans by themselves are meaningless. It is the *action* resulting from the plans which matters. That is why we get people to write down their targets. It makes them more likely to act.

To translate the BACTA into action, you and your distributors should use a weekly diary, where you schedule all the actions to which you have committed yourself in your BACTA targets.

You can also use a single sheet Monthly Planner (see *Target Success!*). This is not used for specific appointments: it is too small for that. Its purpose is to give you what a weekly diary cannot—a balanced monthly overview of your level of activity under the headings of:

- Strategy Meetings
- Retailing Visits
- Contacting Calls
- Two-to-Ones
- BOMs/Sizzles/Trainings.

The Monthly Planner also gives you an incentive to fill up the month ahead with productive work!

6. Will they commit to doing a proper Contact List?

The Contact List is the foundation document for planning, which is why you should never Work With anyone unless they have a proper Contact List: i.e. a list with at least a hundred names.

The whole question of how to prepare Contact Lists is covered in Chapter 8 of *Get Off To A Winning Start*, and in *Target Success!*

Should you help people make out their contact list?

Some people think it is a waste of your valuable time to help people draw up a Contact List. I disagree. Given that it is so important, I think it is a good idea to Work With your people on drawing up their list, even though it is very time-consuming:

- It ensures that it is done. Is it better to spend a few hours helping someone with their list, or to see all the time you have invested in sponsoring them wasted because they will not make one out?
- With your greater experience, you will be able to prompt them to remember more names
- It increases the rapport between you and gets you both into the *Working With* habit
- According to the Theory of Duplication, if you do this exercise with them, they are more likely to do the same with their people.

Now, give your commitment to match their efforts

Explain that this is *their* business but, if they give you these Six Commitments, you will help them to build it. But you will only build it *with* them, not *instead of* them. In other words, your commitment to them is to match your efforts to theirs. If they are going all-out in the time they committed to, so will you. But if they are half-hearted then you will not put yourself out.

Chapter 18

More Tips For Winning Teachers

What separates a winning teacher from an ordinary one is often in the tips used to come across better to people, mostly helping you to be a better ACTTER. I will wind up this section on being a winning teacher by giving you some more useful tips on how to do this.

Assume new distributors know nothing

It is demoralising for new people if you assume they know something they do not. People do not like to admit ignorance and, worse, you will make them feel inadequate.

How much did you know when you started? We can all too easily forget that there was a time when *we* knew nothing about the business, either! Always try to remember what it was like for you when you started, and you won't **go far** wrong.

So, until you know how much a new distributor knows, assume that it is up to *you* to show them *everything*.

Some of your distributors may have considerably more conventional business experience than you, and may well have reached the top of their previous careers. Don't be overawed by this; they may well have been the experts in their old occupation but *you* are the expert in this one—and don't be afraid to say so if it becomes necessary. No matter how much knowledge they have of other things, unless they have been in network marketing before, they will know *nothing* about this industry.

Treat every new distributor as if they are going to 'make it'

A run of drop-outs or people who sign up and insist, despite your every effort, on Going Off-Track and 'doing their own thing', can sometimes make you cynical towards new distributors.

If you allow yourself to feel resigned to 'going through the motions' with new people, this will communicate itself subconsciously to them. If their sixth sense tells them that you think they will drop out, they are half-way to doing just that! Remember that *you* cannot tell who will, or who will not succeed. What you can do is to make sure that many *will* fail—by your negative attitude.

Treat every communication with a distributor as a teaching opportunity

This business is unusual in that, every time you are teaching a distributor, whether face-to-face, by phone or in writing, you are also showing them how to teach their people.

According to the Theory of Duplication, your distributors will copy the way *you* handle any given situation, whether you like it or not. If they are going to copy you anyway, it is surely better that you give them good habits to copy, not bad ones!

So, before you deal with any particular situation, ask yourself the question: *Is the way I am about to tackle this situation the way I would want it to duplicate down my network?*

A good habit is to remind your distributors that *every communication is also a teaching opportunity*; before every meeting or at the start of each phone call with one of your people, say something like, 'Remember that what we discuss today, you may want to cover at some point with one of *your* distributors' or, 'Everything you learn today, you must pass onto your distributors' or, 'You may need to handle this problem sometime in the future, so treat this as a teaching session in how to deal with it.'

Some top network marketeers even make the *Two-to-One* a teaching session, not only for the distributor who is accompanying them, *but for the person they are showing the business to, as well!* They say to the contact, 'This meeting could also be your first training session because, if you *do* like what you hear today and decide to come into this business, the way I show you the business will be the best way for you to show the business to *your* contacts. Of course, if you decide that the business is *not* for you, that will not apply.'

Don't teach how you would do it, teach the best way for your new distributor to do it

We are all different and different people will do the same job in different ways depending on their talents, skills, character, background and experience.

An obvious example is how people say things. A distributor's choice of words should be what sounds natural coming from them, not what may sound right coming from you. This is particularly important when you are helping someone to prepare suitable scripts for the Get-Active phone calls or for dealing with objections.

Oh, shut up!

'Beneficent salutations. I am in attendance to exhibit the multifarious desiderata of a cerebrally stimulating métier.'

The same is true of the Two-to-One. You may be much more articulate than the distributor you are teaching—or they may be much more articulate then you; and perhaps one of you has a much quieter personality than the other, or one is humorous and the other serious. The result is that, although the structure or framework of the Two-to-One should not change, you will present yourselves differently within it.

Never point out problems until you know the answer

There are few things more destructive than saying to someone that they have a problem—but you don't know what to do about it!

Until it is pointed out, people are very often unaware that they have a problem so, as far as they are concerned, there *was* no problem until you mentioned it! But, by bringing it to their attention without having a solution for it, you have definitely created a problem and, because you have no solution, you will have done an excellent job of undermining their confidence.

If you do not know the solution to a problem, the best thing to do is to keep quiet about it until you have had a chance to work one out or discuss it with an upline.

Think before you speak

Not only does this avoid the problem we have just discussed, it is always best to think out the *simplest* and *most effective* way to present your point before you do so. This is all part of playing CUPID. Remember what we said before: *The way you teach them will be the way they teach their people* (the Theory of Duplication) and you want the *simplest* way passed on.

It is very easy to assume that, because a distributor is doing something differently from the way you would do it, they must be doing it wrongly. I think you will agree that, if something is working for them, it is best to leave it alone and find another topic to cover.

It is quite easy to decide whether it is worthwhile to deal with a particular topic or not. Ask yourself, *Will what I am about to say or do actually make them*:

• Faster

• Or more efficient

• Or more effective?

If it does none of those things, leave well alone!

Raise problems in a positive way

Try to avoid using phrases like 'You did that wrong' or, 'That was a mistake'. It is better to say something like, 'Next time you try that, why not have a go at doing it this way?' or, 'Would it improve it if you did it this way?' or, 'Is it worth a go at trying this?'

Showing people how to do something better is usually more effective than showing them how to stop doing something badly; although there are times when the only way you can get through to someone is by doing the latter. If someone simply won't listen, you may have to try shock tactics as a last resort: 'Unless you stop doing that, you are going to have a serious problem with the business!'

Limit criticism and balance with praise

If you think about it, as a winning teacher, you are always looking for the areas in which a distributor needs improvement; not at what they are already doing well. So it can become very easy to start coming out with a catalogue of criticisms or 'areas for improvement'.

This is a great way to make someone who is actually doing an excellent job believe that they are totally incompetent! It is common for managers in traditional business to use the tactic of constant criticism as a way of keeping their

'You did a really good Two-to-One in there. But I noted down just a few areas of improvement which might help you in the future...'

staff in a subservient position. Fortunately, this has no place in network marketing.

Having said that, it is very easy to undermine someone's confidence by mistake! So how do you prevent that from happening?

1. Limit The Teaching Topics

This means that you should choose *only a very few* topics at a time on which to teach. Remember the rule: *Confuse to lose.* If there is a topic which needs a lot of work done on it and which is holding a distributor back, you might decide to deal with that as the only topic.

Which are the best topics to choose? Those which are getting most in the way of a distributor's success. You may find The S.T.A.R. Success Pyramid (page 64) helpful in deciding this.

Because these tend to be big topics, make sure you break them into bite-sized chunks first, so that your new distributor can experience success in tangible, small steps, and second, so that you do not overwhelm them with detail.

2. Get The Basics Right First

This means that you should help a distributor to do a competent *overall* job—getting the 'broad brush strokes' in—before becoming involved in nitty-gritty detail work which will only ever result in small, marginal improvements.

You will notice that I have applied this rule to the S.T.A.R. Leadership Programme. Let's just look at how I tackled the teaching aspects of learning the distributor's job:

1. In *Get Off To A Winning Start*, I made teaching very simple, using broad brush strokes. Basically, teaching consisted of just taking new distributors through the book in their turn, and Working With them

2. In *Breakthrough Sponsoring & Retailing*, I used a medium brush, giving a teacher more to get their teeth into with broad-based concepts like the ACTTER, KISS and CUPID Formulas, which they can pass onto their people and use in their own teaching

3. Now, in this book, we are down to the fine brush work, painting in all the details.

Can you imagine what would happen if you started a new distributor with this book? They would be overwhelmed. But, having had some experience, I don't suppose there is anything here which is 'blowing your mind'... If there is, slow up and read the caution on page 11!

3. Balance With Praise

If people are keen to succeed and are willing to learn, you can always assume that they are doing the best job of which *they* are currently capable. It may seem to you as if they are doing a terrible job, but remember that *their only* agreement with you is: if they Stay On-Track (possibly with the refinement of the Six Planning Commitments—as discussed in the previous chapter), you *will* help them to achieve the standards they are going to need to succeed.

The 'A' of being an ACTTER is that you are accountable to people to help them succeed. There is nothing there about how good they have to be by any given time! So, as well as giving them the respect they deserve for doing the best they can (the 'R' of being an ACTTER), *you must make them feel good about something.* Tell them what they are doing best.

We are talking here, of course, about the value of Patience, one of the Six Winning Attitudes. Handled in the right way, some of your people who start out the worst can often turn out to be the best—if they have a Bulldozer Mentality. But they *definitely* will not if you do not nurture them properly.

Show respect for a distributor's sphere of influence

Everyone likes to feel that the boundaries of their territory are being respected. Even if you are teaching a new distributor, they are still the 'managing director' of their own business; so confirm their status as the head of their group when you are in the presence of their distributors or contacts.

Some of us have massive egos but this is the time to lock them away! If you are attending a distributor's sizzle, a BOM or a training run by them, try not to take over, difficult though that sometimes is! Defer to them, make it clear that they are the 'boss' for the occasion. Ask them what they would like you to do, then stick to it. Whether you feel it or not, show them the respect they deserve for being the leader of their group.

If you do not do this, if you tend to 'take over', your distributors will not want you at their meetings and you will undermine their people's confidence in their leader. But, if you do treat them with respect, if you respect their sphere of influence, you will build great loyalty, you will always be welcome and, most important of all, you will have helped to confirm the confidence of their people in them as a group leader.

Be consistent in your behaviour

Teachers who show mood-swings or who keep changing policies depending on what they heard yesterday are very unsettling to a new distributor! New people learn much more quickly, and develop greater confidence in you, if you get them into an established pattern and routine and if they get used to you always being an ACTTER.

Be an example of what you are teaching: set high standards for yourself

This is a professional business so you should look, and be, professional. Some people think it puts them in a position of importance to roll up late for meetings, but that is a trick for conventional business. In our business it is just sloppy. The simple rule is *never* to be late.

Although there are far fewer rules and procedures laid down by the company in network marketing than in traditional business, there still *are* rules and procedures so it is important that you give an example by following them.

This, of course, means that you must *Practise what you preach*. Unlike in conventional business, *Do what I say, not what I do* does not work because, according to the Theory of Duplication, you will be teaching your people to do the same thing when *they* start teaching.

Before a Two-to-One, decide who will do what... then STICK to it

This is the 'C' of playing CUPID: *Clarify The Agenda*. Before you start any teaching session (including Working With) and, particularly before each Two-to-One, agree what is going to happen. Distributors learn much more quickly if they have an agenda to follow.

It is very tempting for you, as a teacher, to take over the Two-to-One. Not only might distributors find this infuriating but, unless you let them do as much as possible as quickly as possible, they are not going to learn and you will be encouraging the problem of Dependency (page 25).

The hardest time to hold yourself back is when you can see it all going wrong for a distributor. The argument is that, unless you intervene to rescue the situation, there is no chance of sponsoring that contact. Apart from that, you would be pretty hard-hearted if sympathy did not make you want to step in to save your distributor from further embarrassment.

But, in fact, taking over the Two-to-One is not the way to handle this situation:

- The best way for your distributors to learn how to get *out of* situations is to get *into* them in the first place! If they don't handle it well, you can show them a better way afterwards. It is better to lose one contact now than, perhaps, many later
- You are, again, encouraging Dependency if your distributors realise that you will step in to save them.

The best way for new distributors to LEARN is to let them DO

People learn much more from *doing* than they do from *listening*. This is why Working With is so much more effective than Arm's Length Training.

Resist the temptation to do too much yourself just because you lack the Patience to explain what you want done. Ego can also make you want to do things yourself, rather than letting someone else do it. So can boredom—it is much more interesting to do it yourself than to have to watch someone else for the thousandth time! A good way to keep yourself alert and not be tempted to interrupt through boredom is to take notes which you can use in the discussion with your distributor after the Two-to-One.

Yes, it is quicker to do things yourself in the short-term but the more you make a new distributor do, the quicker they will learn and the sooner you can move on to another new distributor.

If you make your new people do as much as they are capable of (and explain why), they will teach their people in the same way.

But be careful not to go too far. If you make people do things before their confidence or competence levels are ready for them, it will be detrimental and will mean that you actually have to spend more time with that person before they are ready to take over. It is all a question of balance, common sense and sensitivity to how they are coping.

Admit your mistakes—and laugh about them!

By laughing at your mistakes you are showing that you *enjoy* your business (the 'E' of being an ACTTER) and are *having fun!*

Some managers subscribe to the theory that people lose confidence in leaders who make mistakes. The complete opposite is the case. Potentially big business-builders come into network marketing because they (correctly) believe that *anyone* can reach the top; if they stop believing in that possibility, they will drop out. Your distributors must be able feel that they can do what you do and who believes they can copy perfection?

New distributors are often frightened of making mistakes, particularly if they have come from a big organisation where the very worst crime is to make a mistake (the second worst is to admit to it). This can hold back their willingness to just get out and have a go! If they see *you*, their leader, treating mistakes lightly, can you imagine how this lifts a load off their shoulders?

People who are not frightened of making mistakes or of making fools of themselves learn very much more quickly than those who are. The great achievers in life can take the risk of looking foolish; if you are not prepared to do that, you will never release your full potential. The same is true of your people.

> The real failure is not in making a mistake, it is in not 'having a go'. Those who are not prepared to make mistakes never achieve anything

---

The only people who do not make mistakes are the dead!

Leave distributors with self-training aims

Self-training is a very productive tool in the teacher's armoury, yet it is hardly ever used.

After a session of Working With, and as the last thing you do before you leave, discuss with the distributor what the best topic for self-training would be.

This is such a successful technique because it requires the distributor to focus for a period on a particular topic chosen by you. Any subject can be chosen for this treatment: any part of their phone call or Two-to-One technique, any aspect of the way in which a distributor teaches their people or handles contacts at BOMs, the way they run sizzle sessions, public speaking at meetings and Formal Trainings—or anything else you can think of.

Some bad habits can be extremely difficult to break or good ones difficult to acquire—such as developing the habit of Consistency in planning and carrying through their BACTA. Habit-breaking or habit-forming can respond well to an intensive period of self-training.

For most people, self-training aims are an essential apart of developing the right attitude; indeed, it is difficult to think of any other way of doing this which is as quick and effective. Changing attitudes takes us into the realms of personal development and, if you think about it:

Just about every book and training on personal development is seeking to get you to set self-training aims

---

Once a self-training aim is agreed, you should advise the distributor of the best training materials (books, tapes and videos) available to deal with that topic.

In this connection, there are bad books, tapes and videos around and you should make it your business to find out which ones will do your distributors more harm than good. If nothing else, harm is done by the wasted cost of buying them and the wasted time in studying them.

It is one thing to agree a self-training aim with a distributor, it is quite another to get them to do it! In many cases, they will not deliberately omit to carry out self-training aims; these can get forgotten in the midst of all the other things a distributor has to do. This can especially be the case with a new distributor who will not yet have acquired good work habits.

So use Constant Repetition again; make it your business to constantly remind them. Ask how they are getting on with their self-training aim *every time you speak to them*, whether personally or by phone. Once a distributor realises that their self-training aim is going to be discussed at every opportunity, they will soon develop the habit of carrying out whatever activity has been agreed!

Once the purpose of the current self-training aim has been achieved, a new one should be agreed.

No matter how experienced we are, all teachers and leaders should set themselves self-training aims

As you improve and acquire more knowledge and experience, you should find that your self-training aims incline more towards personal development rather than being directly job-related.

Effective teaching should lead to enjoyable action!

Now that we have finished Part II, Be A Winning Teacher, I want to stress two last points:

First, tuition should not replace the attitude of *Urgency in Action*. Its *sole* purpose is to help a distributor to *do* better.

Second, there is a danger that tuition can take the spontaneity and fun out of a job. It shouldn't. Proper tuition should bring *more* success and therefore *more* fun to the business.

Although we have covered a lot of detail, I hope you did not find anything particularly difficult. Anyway, don't worry too much about the detail at this stage. Once you start to practise the craft of being a winning teacher, you will find that everything will soon slot into place. The main thing is to keep reading and rereading this section and comparing it with what you are actually doing with your people.

Very soon, it will all be automatic.

Now we go on to the final part of the book, where we explore the art of winning leadership.

Theory versus practice

As I said on page 97, there is going to be a difference between how much time you *ought* to spend with a new distributor (i.e., until he or she knows as much as you do), and how much time you *can* spend with them, which rapidly reduces as their group grows, requiring you to spend time with new downlines.

There are three solutions to this, all of which you aught to apply:

1. Get them to study this book and the rest of the S.T.A.R. Leadership Programme

2. Keep in frequent phone contact, talking through techniques with them. Confirm these discussions with self-training aims

3. Make discussions on how to teach and lead an important part of sizzles and other meetings. Have regular day seminars on teaching and leading—at least monthly if you can get at least five people attending.

4. In this way, and only in this way, will you get distributors who mature into expert, professional teachers and leaders within three to six months of joining.

Part III
Be A Winning Leader!

Although everyone becomes a leader whether they like it or not the minute they sponsor their first distributor, we have seen that there are two distinct types of leader. If you are a small to medium-sized business-builder, you may prefer to delegate the active leadership of your group to the upline distributors who have chosen to take on active leadership roles. You do this through applying the Figure-of-Eight Attitude, connecting your downlines with your uplines.

However, although you can delegate your active leadership role upline, you cannot expect upline leaders to shoulder your responsibility to Work With your people as a teacher, unless they offer to do this for you.

You may, of course, want to take on a much more positive leadership role. Indeed, if you want a high income or a large group, you will have to. This final section of the book is written primarily for those who want to become active leaders.

But, even if you are not taking on an active leadership role at this stage of your business, you will find great benefit in reading this section, both for running your own group and because you will be more help to your upline active leaders if you understand how they have to do their job.

Chapter 19

As A Leader, What Should Your Management Style Be?

In this chapter, we will take a look at what being a winning leader means, in other words, how you should behave towards your people.

In Chapter 4 we saw that, although your people are all self-employed, the great majority want to be part of a structure and a team. The more experienced network marketing leaders become, the more you will see them behaving like the leaders of conventional businesses. In other words, they create a recognised and acceptable way of doing things for their distributors and they expect their people to follow that path.

Where they differ from the leaders of conventional business is the way in which they handle those who do not conform. A conventional leader uses disciplinary actions; in the final analysis these could be dismissal or termination of contract. A network marketing leader, having discharged the responsibility of showing a distributor the right way of doing things and warning them of what might happen if they don't Stay On-Track, lets them go their own way. One of three things will happen if one of your distributors chooses to Go Off-Track:

• They will fail and drop out

• They will realise the error of their ways and come back to the fold

• By some miracle, they will succeed.

Only in the second case will you, the upline, come back into the equation (although in the third eventuality you will be in the nice position of receiving royalties for doing nothing!)

Be a leader, not a manager! Lead on your feet, not from your butt! Lead from the front!

Managers are the bane of British business. They think they are leaders but they are not; they sit behind desks telling other people what to do but are not prepared to do it themselves. They no longer believe that they must give a good example to their people. They will not lower themselves to 'rolling their sleeves up and getting stuck in'. Their motto is *Do what I say, not what I do.*

Winning leaders are the complete opposite. They lead from the front. They lead by example. They 'muck in', 'roll their sleeves up' and Work With their people. They are always to be seen in the thick of what is going on. They gain the respect of their people because they are seen to share their tribulations with them.

A winning leader has broad shoulders and a small butt, a manager has small shoulders and a big butt. A winning leader looks to the front, a manager looks over their shoulder. There is no room for managers in network marketing—only for leaders

---

If you want to be a winning leader, spend as much time as you can out there with your people, showing them by example how to Work With, be seen at meetings, trainings, sizzles and BOMs and mix with them as much as you can.

If you lead from the front, your people will follow you. If you lead from behind, your people will hang back with you

---

Take responsibility!

Again, don't imitate the managers of conventional business. To them, 'taking responsibility' means, 'I am responsible for any success but *you* are responsible for any failure'! Is anyone else except you going to make your group successful? No. So you might as well accept *total* responsibility for making your success happen.

A winning leader does not worry about how much ability they have

Your people need your *support*, not your *talent*.

The support you give your group will overcome any lack of talent you *think* you might have

---

Actually, if you understand this, you have the one talent that really matters because you understand what the Keystone Law really means—that, if you give your people the framework they need to succeed, *you* will succeed. There are many so-called talented people out there who do not build the size of group they want because they do not understand that:

Your abilities cannot make up for any lack of results in your group, but your group can make up for any apparent lack of ability in you

---

... if you give them the leadership they need.

If, as a winning leader in network marketing, you do not need to do the job better than your people, what abilities *do* you need? The abilities you want are exactly the same as those of a captain, but not a captain of a ship, who needs a different type of relationship with their crew; you are like the captain of a sports team, albeit a very large one! What do the players on a team want of their captain?:

- No-one in the team expects the captain to do a better job than they do, but they *do* expect him to have a better *attitude* to the job than they do, which means that, although he cannot do the job better than they can, he tries harder than they do: he trains harder, works harder, is more committed to success than they are, is more competitive than they are

- They do not expect the captain to do a better job than they do but they do want him to help *them* to be better at what they do

- They expect him to *know* more about the job than they do, even if he cannot *do* it better

- They expect the captain be loyal to them and to support them when they need it

- They expect the captain to listen to what they say but then, having made a decision, have the courage to stick to it, no matter how unpopular it is. But they also expect him to do what is best for the team, which means having the wisdom to change that decision if it becomes clear that it is the wrong one

- They expect the captain to lead from the front. If he leads from the front, they will follow him; if he does not, they will lag behind with him. So they want him to show them the way, to lay down the ground rules, not be to better than them at what *they* do

- What gains the team's respect is the willingness of the captain to get onto the playing field with them, to be in the thick of the game with them, to share their triumphs and disappointments, not to be better than they are.

You need exactly the same attributes as the captain of that team. It is being seen to be doing and sharing which are important, not how well you do it.

As a winning leader, how tough do you need to be?

Many people opt out of leadership because they believe that an effective leader has to be tough and uncaring and they would rather be, in their terms, more 'human'. But there does not have to be this conflict because toughness should only ever mean being a straight, honest talker and being Urgent in Action.

Toughness should be used only to help people to get the best out of themselves. If toughness goes beyond this into callousness, which means using rather than helping people, it is unacceptable. It also means that a leader no longer accepts their responsibilities to their people and this is where unethical management practices creep in.

In the same way, caring should mean understanding people so that you can 'manage' them best to motivate them to get the results they want. If caring means sympathising with people who are not doing their best, it becomes weakness. It is weakness, not caring, which results in not being prepared to take unpleasant but necessary actions and not confronting unpalatable truths in *their* interests when it is needed.

> True responsibility to your people means being tough when you need to be, caring when you need to be and knowing the difference

So, in many situations, true kindness means being tough. Although they may sometimes go too far and lose people, tough leaders will always get better results because they push people to the limit. The over-caring person will never lose anyone as a result of their management style but then they never push anyone to stretch their limits.

So being a winning leader is not the same as 'riding rough-shod' over people.

There are two sorts of leader: those who think the organisation is there for their benefit, and those who think they are there for the organisation's benefit

---

A lot of your people, and perhaps you yourself, will be used to conventional organisations which are full of managers who think that the organisation is there for their benefit. These managers do ride roughshod over people. They are not interested in finding out what is actually best for the organisation, but only what is best for themselves; the result is that they do not listen to their staff and they try to impose their views on people, instead of finding out the best way to get the job done.

If you approach the leadership of your group in this way, you will be lucky to build a group which survives. I am not saying it cannot be done, because this is how some big business-builders do lead their groups, but I will show you a better and easier way. If you want to apply the Keystone Law (which means that getting the best out of your group *is* what is best for you), see yourself as the opposite to con-ventionally trained managers—see yourself as being there *for the benefit of the group.*

Unlike a conventional manager, if you take the attitude that you are there to *serve* your group, you will become more interested in finding out what your people need, rather than in imposing your own views. Your decision-making will also be entirely different: instead of deciding for yourself what the right decision is and then imposing it, you will listen with a very open mind to other peoples' views before making up your mind.

Where the toughness comes in is that:

- You must be tough enough to listen carefully and with an open mind *even to people you think are wrong.* Listen to *everybody.* Very often, it is the newest people with a fresh point of view who will notice the flaws which everyone else has become blind to, or who see the creative solution which experienced people miss because it is outside the accepted way of doing things

- If distributors cannot succeed unless they are prepared to Stay On-Track, you must be tough enough not to waste your time with anyone who chooses a different route and firm enough to ensure that your leaders and teachers do the same

- You must be tough enough, once the decision is made, to make sure it is carried out. People who do not agree with your final decision will accept it much more readily if they feel that you gave them a fair chance to put their point of view

- If the decision does not get the results you and the group expect, you must be tough enough to reopen the debate and, if necessary, admit you were mistaken and change your opinion.

Sticking with a course of action that is obviously not going to work is not tough, it is stupid—or weak because you cannot admit that you were wrong. It takes a tough person, but a person genuinely working for the good of the group, to say, 'My decision did not work, it is time to find another solution'.

The great thing about network marketing is that you can actually look around and see effective leaders in action. You will notice that people who understand the value of listening to successful distributors (the 'L' of The Training LLAWR), will gravitate towards those leaders who are straight-talking; they want leaders who will 'tell it as it is'.

You will also see group leaders who are so anxious to be liked that they find it impossible to be straight and honest with their people. These are the people who are not prepared to accept the harsher realities of Staying On-Track and let their people believe it is possible to succeed by taking a different route. This is serious because they are responsible for the failure of people who trusted them to give the right guidance. With this in mind, weak leaders should recognise that they are no better than callous leaders because each causes equal damage to their people.

Yes, you do need to be tough if that means caring enough about your people to be straight and honest with them, and to accept the responsibility which goes with the authority of leadership. That responsibility can be discharged only by finding out what is *actually* needed for success in this great industry—not what you hope, would like or prefer to be needed—and making sure you pass this onto your people.

Your job as a leader is to light the *right* way

Accept that wonderful and privileged responsibility and you will be, not just a winning leader, but a *great* leader, deserving of the respect, the loyalty and, above all, the *success* which you *will* get.

Earlier, I said that the definition of Winning Leadership is:

Training + Direction + Motivation

A winning leader is good at all three, so we will now look at each of them in turn, starting with training.

Chapter 20

Winning Leaders Control Training For Their Group

Winning Leadership = **TRAINING** + Direction + Motivation

We have looked in detail at how you should carry out your job as a winning teacher. We are now going to look at training not through your eyes as a winning *teacher* but through your eyes as a winning *leader*. As a winning leader, there is a wider aspect to training: how you get your training methods and standards through to the whole group rather than, in your function as a teacher, concentrating on individual distributors in the group.

Lack of Arm's Length Training is not usually a problem in network marketing. But, as a winning leader, *your* aim will be to ensure that the accent is heavily on Working With and that Arm's Length Trainings are used only to support Working With, not instead of it. You will also want to ensure that your distributors follow the Steps of Training (page 73) as a matter of habit, that Two-to-Ones, not One-to-Ones, are the norm and that your people are ACTTERS who play CUPID.

It is one thing to attain high standards and check that only good teaching habits are being practised when your group is small. It is quite another to keep them that way when the group gets large or during periods of fast growth in your distributor base.

When leaders achieve the levels of income and lifestyles they have been working for, a new danger will threaten—*complacency*. And with complacency comes falling standards, bad habits and people talking a good act instead of doing a good job.

You have two ways of avoiding these problems:

1. Constant Repetition of the lessons of network marketing

2. Making sure that you and your leaders constantly lead from the front, lead by example and focus on Working With.

Part II, *Be A Winning Teacher*, concentrated mainly on Working With because that is the primary function of a winning teacher. However, Arm's Length Training does have an extremely important part to play in its own right and we covered this on page 56. Let's now take a closer look at what is involved.

There are two forms of Arm's Length Training

These are:

• *Formal Training* (also called classroom training), where the trainer decides beforehand what the training agenda is going to be and then presents it in a formal way

• *Reactive Training*, where the trainer reacts to the specific needs or problems of an individual or group. Training over the phone and the confusingly named 'one-to-one' meetings with a distributor (as opposed to Two-to-Ones with a contact) are mostly of a reactive nature. Sizzle sessions are also an important part of Reactive Training and we will cover these in the next chapter.

Trainings are often run before or after BOMs. I do not personally subscribe to this because I think that BOMs are primarily for guests. Trainings can get in the way of guests being properly looked after—and it is not always the right tactic to have guests sitting in on a training.

Formal Trainings can be called 'nuts and bolts' trainings to differentiate them from motivational meetings. Whether formal training or motivational meeting, they can be called *seminars*, and can take place in a variety of formats: one hour, two hours, one day, two days, evenings, week-ends. You can also have regular weekly or monthly seminars or occasional 'one-off' meetings.

As a leader, you can organise seminars yourself or you can motivate the distributors in your business to support seminars being run by other groups (crossline or upline)—or both.

Many leaders like to 'keep their distributors to themselves'

These are the 'lone wolves' we looked at on page 37. They discourage their downlines from co-operating with other groups and encourage insularity. If you want to be as successful as you can be, theirs are not the ranks to join.

Good teamwork does not just apply upline and downline, it applies crossline and into other groups as well

---

Do you need to organise your own group BOMs, trainings and events to be a winning leader?

For ease of reference, we will lump together BOMs, trainings and other meetings as 'events'.

Please note that we are *not including sizzle sessions as an event* because, once their group starts to build, every distributor should be running their own 'closed' meetings or sizzle sessions (that is, restricted to invited downlines). We will have a look at sizzles in the next chapter.

In the early stages, you do not need to set up your own events. In fact you should not if there are other *good* events in the geographical areas where your group is active, because you can link yourself and your group into those.

Once a group reaches a certain size, its leaders do tend to look at setting up their own group events. If other good events are available it is not essential, although there probably is a benefit if you intend to become a big business-builder.

Before you decide whether to organise your own events, there are some points to bear in mind:

• One of the great things about network marketing is that distributors co-operate in helping each other to build their businesses, *even if they are in different groups in the network*. Any action which turns co-operation between distributors or groups into competition is simply unacceptable

• Events need to be of a certain size before they can generate the *group dynamic* or *group momentum* so essential to their success. Therefore, the rule is that local distributors from all groups in a given geographic area should co-operate on one event until the attendance is big enough to support another. So it is not acceptable to set up an event in an area if, by doing this, you will make an existing one unsustainable. When the other local event is big enough to create its own group momentum without the people you will draw away from it, then it is perfectly acceptable to start your own

• If other events in the area are not of a high standard, as a winning leader, you have no option: you must either offer to help improve them, or start your own. Inactivity is not an option—there is no such thing as a winning leader with a badly trained or motivated group!

• There is no point in organising a *worse* event than another one available in the area. That is vanity! Yours must be at least as good as, if not better than, *all* others in the area. If it is not, swallow your pride, close down your event and tie in with the best one around

• Just as *your* people should be welcomed at events held by other groups, so distributors from *other* groups and, if relevant, their guests must be made welcome at yours.

What if you are a bad public speaker?

There is no such thing—there are only good public speakers and badly *trained* public speakers. I am sure you are getting heartily sick of my saying that *anyone* can learn all these skills, but it actually is true in network marketing! ... *Anyone* can learn to become a good speaker at events.

There are two sorts of speaker needed:

• *Trainers who play CUPID*, presenting training simply and logically, so that their audience can learn in the easiest possible way

• *Motivators*. More ability is required to be a good motivational speaker but, if a person is prepared to speak from the heart with Pride (one of the Six Winning Attitudes), and can learn to love their audience, they can acquire the skill. This may not make them a *great* motivational speaker (the difference between the good and the great is that the great speakers have *charisma*, which we discussed before), but they can, nevertheless, make people feel good about themselves—and that is what counts.

In any case, the point is not whether you could become a good public speaker but whether you would *enjoy* speaking week-in, week-out at events. If not, don't do more than you must to be seen to be leading from the front! There are plenty of other distributors who are willing to speak. *You* organise, *you* decide the course content and, in the main, *they* speak. It is a good tactic to invite speakers from other groups within the network because the more that different groups co-operate at local level, the more each will benefit.

The important thing is to control the *quality* of what is going on—in this case, making sure that the distributors in your business have the best possible trainings for themselves, the best possible BOMs to take their guests to and the most motivating events possible.

How To Make Your Events As Effective As Possible!

Remember who they are for!

Events should only be held if they will benefit your *distributors* although, in some cases such as BOMs, this actually means that the interests of their *guests* should come first. Events are not showcases for your vanity or for the egos of your group leaders or speakers:

Plan the whole event and the course content to answer the needs of your distributors or guests, not to cater for the egos of you and your group leaders

---

In all events, the slowest learners and the least experienced are the people who matter most

This is supposed to be a simple business. Speakers who do not ensure that the slowest learners and the least experienced have understood are not playing CUPID and have already started to complicate things.

Therefore, make sure that all content is aimed at helping the slowest learners and the least experienced to understand it.

Use a variety of speakers

For BOMs, trainings and in-house events, try to get speakers from both sexes, with a variety of ages and backgrounds.

If the event is one at which guests are present, variety helps to ensure that if a guest does not relate to one speaker, they may warm to another. It also proves what they have been told: that *successful distributors come from all sorts of backgrounds*.

If you are running a training session for new distributors, it boosts their confidence to see a variety of speakers because you are showing them in action that successful network marketeers do, indeed, come from all sorts of background. This is especially powerful if they can identify with one of the speakers.

At trainings, having a variety of speakers serves another very important purpose. Trainings generally involve a lot of content. It takes a great deal out of one person to have to present content in a carefully simplified way for too long. More importantly, there is only so much the listeners can take in. For them, a variety of speakers helps to break the strain of concentration—a change is as good as a rest.

But do not delay an event just because you cannot get enough speakers. Remember that we said events are held for the benefit of your people; if it is more valuable for them to have a session held by one person than to have no session at all, then hold it.

If having the 'right' number of speakers means including some bad ones, it may be better for those attending if you stick to the better speakers, even if this means having fewer than you would like. There is no set answer on this, it will depend on the situation at the time.

The only exception to the rule of variety is when you invite an outside expert, well-known personality or great motivational speaker to talk to your people.

Make sure your speakers play CUPID

In the introduction, remember 'C'—*Clarify the agenda.*

Where BOMs are concerned, they are a complete waste of time if guests cannot understand what is going on.

Where trainings are concerned, can I remind you that Arm's Length Trainings must only be used *in support* of, not *instead of*, Working With. If a training seminar is going to last for several hours—and most will—the *simpler* your speakers make the content, the *more* will be remembered when those who attended go back to Work With their sponsors or uplines.

Many distributors and guests, possibly the majority, do not come from good educational backgrounds. They, and their needs, must be respected. Some topics are not easy to explain, but that is no excuse for speakers making them even more difficult to understand by not playing CUPID.

Avoid questions!

In the early days, it will often be necessary to use inexperienced distributors as speakers, and BOMs are regularly used to give someone their first taste of public speaking. So can I suggest you do not allow questions unless *all* the speakers can handle them (it is no good explaining that Mary can take questions, but Fred can't). Having seen many a poor devil caught out by an innocent question they could not answer and many a BOM ruined by an awkward guest, it is not worth the risk!

Instead, in the introduction, ask people who are attending to note down their questions and put them to experienced distributors in the breaks.

Make sure training seminars follow the Steps of Training (page 73)

This does not mean that each speaker must follow all the steps of this formula because you may decide that two or even three speakers cover one topic. In this case, what you must ensure is that, between them, the speakers have followed all the Steps.

The Step that is most commonly forgotten is: 'Then **check** *they understand'.* Yet, of all the Steps, *it is the most important.* If you think about it, there is no purpose in training except to make people understand! If they do not, *the confusion you have caused will have done more harm than good.*

Inject the occasional humour, light relief, illustrative story or real-life example

It is not necessary for every speaker to be humorous. Many *good* training speakers are not. But humour at periodic intervals during the event definitely helps so try to intersperse speakers who are not humorous with those who are.

Whether humorous or not, *any* speaker can tell a story or give a real-life example to illustrate a point. These are essential to keeping the audience's concentration going for longer and for getting a message across in a simple, telling way. They also help a speaker who is having to take a longer than usual 'stint' because of a shortage of speakers.

Use visual aids

Some speakers think that visual aids are crutches for poor speakers. Nonsense. No matter how brilliant the speaker, *good* visual aids will make them better. It is easier for listeners to understand a topic if it is shown as well as explained. That is why visual aids are an absolutely vital part of playing CUPID. In fact, if a speaker does not use visual aids, they are not KISSing!

People remember far more of what they see *and* hear than of what they only hear

---

Visual aids must be of good quality

You are projecting the image of a high-level business. Tatty visual aids do not support that image.

Good visual aids need not be expensive. The most common presentation tool is the Overhead Projector or OHP. Any computer with a laser or ink-jet printer can produce quality OHP acetates (but be sure to buy the right kind or you can damage the printer). Alternatively, most copy shops can produce acetates from your paper masters at reasonable cost. Bearing in mind that OHP acetates are a 'one-off' expenditure, it costs only a little more to have them on varied coloured backgrounds and properly mounted on board frames.

Speakers do not *have* to write in public on flip-charts, acetates or boards, so only let them do so if they have good
writing. If they do not, get someone who is a good writer to
prepare their visual aids in advance.

Choose a good venue

It is not convincing to talk about a high-level business
from a cold, seedy bar! If you cannot afford a good loca-
tion, talk to your own distributors or leaders from other
groups about sharing the cost.

Can everyone see, hear, and be comfortable?

Check that those at the back of the room can hear. Those
with hearing difficulties should be offered a seat at the
front and those with sight difficulties should be offered a
seat where they can best overcome their problem.

Apart from this, the common faults are that people cannot
see the speaker or the visual aids without craning their
necks, or that the visual aids are too small or too unclear to
be seen by people at the back. For the same reason, pastel
colours should only be used for the *background* of a visual
aid, never for the *text*. For OHP acetates use only clear or a
light tint as a background colour. Avoid using the dark colour schemes you will find in many software packages—
these are intended for use with 35mm slide projectors
which have a stronger light. Text should always be black or
very strong colours, to make it stand out.

With regard to comfort, particularly for a long event, people should be able to move sideways without digging their
neighbours in the ribs. They should also be able to
straighten out their legs underneath the seat in front.
Watch the temperature, too. Over-hot means drowsiness,
over-cold means lack of concentration!

Learn from the organisers of the good events

So often, group leaders start up their own events and then
make the same mistakes everyone else has made before!

Don't automatically assume that you can improve on another speaker's way of presenting—they could be doing it that way for a reason. For instance, a lot of what you hear may sound so simple or obvious to you as to be not worth mentioning. But the speaker may well know that these points are not obvious to many people coming into the business. If you miss them out, you will not be KISSing and playing CUPID. You will also not taking account of two points I made earlier:

- In all events, the slowest learners and the least experienced people are those who matter most
- Trainings and events are for the benefit of the distributors (or their guests), not for you.

The responses to my earlier series of books produced good examples of people who, because *they* knew something, thought it must be obvious to others. Some criticised the series for being too simplistic but I had many more phone calls from distributors who thanked me for making them so simple! I hope that the least experienced among you find this much more comprehensive series equally simple to follow, because it is for *you* I write and run my trainings, not for those who find everything 'obvious'.

So, if you are not sure why content is included in a seminar, or why it is being presented in a particular way, why not ask the organiser or speaker?

Learn from other people's mistakes: go and talk to them first—and, if you are starting a regular BOM or training, why not ask if they could come and help on the first few? A conscientious trainer will welcome the chance to learn from you just as much as vice-versa. Out of the shared experience, they might just find ways to improve their own BOMs or trainings.

Make suits or business clothes the required dress code

There are bound to be serious business or professional people at the event. Guests may take along a professional adviser. Either way, appearances *do* count and none of these people are impressed by casual clothes at a business meeting.

At BOMs, you may consider the policy at many well-run meetings of having a distributor at the door who will turn away improperly dressed people. To avoid embarrassment, instruct distributors to make it abundantly clear to their guests that they must be properly dressed.

Start on time

If the meeting starts late, not only does this look unprofessional but those attending may lose some of their enthusiasm.

Is it right that the great majority of keen people, who made sure they arrived on time, are held up for a minority of less keen people who have shown a lack of respect for the organisers and the event?

This is particularly important at BOMs where guests can get very fidgety if the start is delayed; it also puts an extra strain on hosts who are trying to keep their guests happy.

Run your events for the many who are ready to start on time, not for the few who are not

---

Have a policy on late arrivals

No matter how quietly they enter, late arrivals are a disruption, particularly for an inexperienced speaker. You may consider a policy that any people arriving late are not allowed in; many well-run meetings have a distributor on the door who actually stops late arrivals from entering.

Have a policy on early leavers

Leaving early is an act of discourtesy to speakers and organisers, most of whom are not paid and are giving up their own time. Even though unpaid, are *they* allowed to leave before the meeting finishes?

Guests at a BOM or new distributors at a training can be disconcerted by seeing people drift off early, no matter what the reason. Meetings often run over time. People attending should be advised to allow for this.

Again, many well-run meetings have a policy that, if a person cannot stay until the end, they do not come. They can always attend a later event.

> **Run your events for the many who will stay to the end, whatever time that is, not the few who can't**

Should you charge for events?

Top distributors can disagree quite strongly over the right policy for charging and some companies have strict rules on the issue. My comments assume that your company does gives latitude on this subject. Having said that, different events require a different approach:

BOMs

These are the 'heart' of the business and you therefore need to encourage your people to support them as much as possible, whether they have a guest or not. So any charges should do no more than cover costs. There are three forms of BOM:

1. A BOM can be a distributor inviting a small group of their own contacts to their own home. Clearly, this is going to be at the host distributor's own cost

2. A BOM can be an upline holding a meeting in their own home and asking selected distributors in their group to bring guests. It is only fair that the upline asks those distributors who do attend to pay their share of whatever

costs are involved; but it would not be normal to expect a profit on the event

3. As a leader, you may decide to hold a regular weekly BOM in a local venue such as a nice hotel. Again, because you want as many distributors as possible to attend as often as possible, you should not aim to profit from the event but it is acceptable to cover your costs.

There are four ways to cover the costs of 'open' BOMs:

1. Charge a fee to every distributor who attends but guests come free, *or* guests of distributors from your own group come free but guests of distributors from other groups are paid for

2. Charge a fee for everyone who attends (although a sensible distributor would pay for their own guests!)

3. Expect every distributor who has reached a certain level on the compensation plan to pay a fee but those who have not yet reached that position come free. This helps those who have not yet had a chance to earn to get their business going before they get involved in BOM costs. Bear in mind that you *want* these distributors to make a habit of attending at least one BOM a week (as their BACTA target). Having to pay an entrance fee, at a time when they may have no money, could militate against that

4. Distributors below a certain position in your own group come free but *all* distributors from other groups pay a fee.

If you have speakers or distributors from another group helping you, members of their group should be treated in exactly the same way as yours for charging purposes.

Ask the people who are helping you to run BOMs to keep an eye out for distributors who avoid paying the fee by waiting in the bar while their guests attend the meeting. If one of your distributors is involved, ask their upline to have a word with them; if they persist, get their distributorship terminated because they are a terrible example to have in your group. If they belong to another group, take the matter up with their group leader.

Motivational events, i.e., events other than trainings

These tend to be of a less frequent and much bigger nature. Unlike BOMs, trainings and other, smaller events, these are not always open to members of other groups. They are proper *occasions*: monthly, quarterly or annual conventions of large numbers of distributors. Some are profit-making ventures, others are not. It does not seem to make much difference either way to turn-out (*provided that the charge is reasonable*) because people want to be involved anyway.

Of course, if you want to put on such an event and cannot afford to fund it yourself with contributions from any other leaders involved, you will have to charge distributors an entry fee.

Trainings

There are three schools of thought about whether you should charge for trainings:

• Some say they should be free, to encourage all distributors to attend

• Some say that you should charge only a nominal fee to cover the cost of administration and overheads

• Some say they should be made into profitable ventures for the organisers.

The argument sometimes put forward by distributors who complain about the cost of trainings, and by some corporate teams, is that the leaders who run them are investing in the future of their businesses and they are going to recoup this investment by higher earnings and a faster growing group.

That of course is true—but they are missing the point that trainings help just as much to build distributors' *own* groups as they do the leaders' so, if the argument is that leaders should fund the costs of trainings, the same argument should apply to the distributors using them. Why should leaders have to subsidise distributors on top of the considerable commitment and work involved in organising and manning trainings?

My experience is that those who complain most about the cost of trainings do not themselves help or speak at them. They simply take advantage of what is offered and it is only right that they should pay for the privilege. Complainers are more likely to drop out anyway, so there is no business sense in subsidising them.

As this is a business for people who run their own businesses, there is nothing wrong with the concept of paying for the privilege of learning from the hard-earned experience of the group leaders.

Leaders give up a lot of time to run trainings and speak at them—time which other distributors not so committed are able to spend on their own business-building. Apart from BOMs, the most regular events are weekly trainings for new distributors. These are half- or, more often, full-day affairs and are best run on Saturdays or Sundays, which means that organisers and speakers also have to give up their week-ends.

It is claimed that trainings should be free or low-cost to encourage more distributors to attend. My belief is that the extra distributors who might come because it is free or low-cost are those most likely to drop out and that the more serious distributors will attend anyway. However you should have an arrangement for those facing genuine financial hardship.

Where I *can* see the difference between a free/low-cost training and one which makes a profit for the leaders is in the quality of the training. There is no doubt that, in general, those which are run with the intention of being profitable are very much better than those which are not. There are some exceptions to this but not many because, although low-cost trainings attract the most altruistic speakers, profitable ones attract the best. Distributors therefore only get the best deal from a low-cost training if the most altruistic speakers also happen to be the best—which does not happen often!

There is also no doubt that people get more out of something if they have to pay for it than if they get it free. Certainly, where trainings are concerned, it is well proven in other fields that people take them a lot more seriously if they have had to pay. Even the Bible says:

> *'People under instruction should always contribute*
> *something to the support of the man who is instructing*
> *them' (Galatians, 6:6).*

So, if you apply the first rule we gave above—what benefits the distributors attending (as opposed to those running it) most—it is the *costlier* trainings from which they benefit most! This may seem surprising, but it is borne out by observation.

Chapter 21

Winning Leaders Control Their Group BOMs And Sizzles!

In the last chapter, although we looked at events in general, we touched on BOMs only in so far as they had points in common with those other events. In this chapter, we look at the points which particularly affect BOMs. We will also look closely at sizzles.

How important are BOMs?

Not all companies promote the use of BOMs. If they do, the BOM is usually made the central point of the sponsoring process. It then becomes a watershed because all prior activity is aimed at getting or 'inviting' the guest to attend. After it, if a contact says 'Yes', the emphasis changes and activity is aimed at getting their new business up and running.

Where BOMs are promoted, they also become the public face or the 'showcase' of the company; indeed, some companies call their BOMs, *'showcases'*. Potential distributors are going to judge your business, not on its *actual* potential in any objective sense, but on what they *see* of it and how they value what they see. To put it at its simplest:

A guest makes their decision, *not* on the
opportunity itself, but on the sponsor, on
the people they meet, on the other
distributors they see and on the BOM itself

It is therefore senseless to have BOMs which are anything other than as attractive and professional as possible. This might seem like common sense, but you would be surprised at how many BOMs seem deliberately designed to put off a serious person! Because the great majority are run by distributors, rather than by the company, you will find great variations in the quality of BOMs even within the same company and—unless the group leader exercises control over them—within the same *group* in the company.

For this reason, if you are intending to take a guest to a BOM you have not been to before (perhaps because it is in a different part of the country), it is wise to check it out first either by attending yourself or by getting someone whose judgement you trust to have a look.

How should you structure your own BOM?

Keep It Short and Straightforward, which is another version of the KISS Formula: 30 to 40 minutes is quite long enough. The business is being sold as a simple business. The accent all the way through must be on how simple it is—*anyone* can do it. If the BOM goes on for too long, or if any speaker is allowed to get away from a very simple approach, the BOM will lose some of its effect.

Stick to *why* guests should do the business (in other words, what might be in it for them), not *how* they should do it. This is one of the basic rules of winning sponsoring; it is therefore as relevant to the speakers at a BOM as it is to a sponsor. This helps to keep the presentation short and simple.

In particular, never discuss the compensation plan in any detail. Most are extremely complicated and the ramifications are often not fully understood by experienced distributors, never mind new ones! You should, however, explain the self-promotion system, how people choose for themselves where they want to be on the plan, and what people can earn, because these are three big selling points to potential distributors.

The BOM has only two purposes:

1. To give guests enough information to go back to their sponsors for the final discussion to decide whether they should come into the business or not

2. To give guests the reassurances they want about:

– The company, its management and its financial status

– The product, how it compares in price and quality with its competitors, its saleability and the marketplace

– What network marketing is. Some BOMs do not mention network marketing, preferring to promote only a 'business opportunity'. There is nothing particularly for or against this provided that it is recognised that, at some stage, a new distributor has got to know and *become proud of the fact* that it is network marketing

– The ethics of both the company and the industry

– 'Can I do it?'

– 'What support will you give me to do it?'

If any of your BOM's content does not fulfil one of these criteria, think again about whether it should be included.

Guests often look at more than one opportunity: some may be dubious and largely sold on 'hype'; others, ethical or not, will be hell-bent on 'selling the deal'. It creates a lot of confidence in your integrity, and makes a refreshing change, if you adopt a different approach. First, make it very clear that a guest's decision about whether or not to get involved is a very serious one and the purpose of the meeting is to give them the facts without any pressure, so that they can make the right decision for *themselves*. Second, stress that, in making such a decision, they need to bear three very important points in mind:

• In the longer term, their business cannot be stronger than the product

• They cannot be more successful than the company they choose.

• If they do come in, a lot of valuable time is going to be given to them by a lot of very busy people, so it is important all round that the right decision is made.

This is very far from *Selling the deal!*

Give your distributors guidelines for BOMs

BOMs are for the benefit of all distributors. You may find some distributors in your group *quite innocently* spoiling it for the others because they do not understand the importance of the occasion. The way to avoid this is to set down some basic guidelines for your group.

To make it easier for you, I have written these guidelines as if you are addressing them to your people, so that you can just copy and issue them:

1. *Support your BOM.* There is nothing more depressing for speakers than to present an opportunity to a tiny audience! Would *you* like to take one of your guests to an almost deserted meeting? BOMs are put on for *your* benefit and the benefit of the distributors in your group, so please support the event and ask your people to do the same. Guests do not realise that most of the people there are distributors, all they see is a lot of people present and a lively buzz going on.

   Whether you have guests or not, you should go to at least one BOM a week (this is why it is included in the Business Activity Agreement) because meetings are an important part of team-building. As the rule states: *No-one ever succeeded by **not** going to meetings.*

   Distributors owe a responsibility to each other. There is a saying: *If you feel bad, you need the meetings but, if you feel good, the meetings need you!* When you are feeling motivated you should always go along, even if you have no guest to take, so that you can share that feeling with others at the meeting who are feeling 'down'. Next week, the roles could be reversed and you could be only too pleased to go to a meeting and have someone help you to rebuild your confidence.

Use meetings to build up a file of distributors who may be useful in the future when you are looking for a *Compatible Distributor* to link up with a guest. Compatible distributors do not have to be in your paylines or even in our group

2. *Invite your guest's spouse or life-partner.* Remember that opposition from spouses or life-partners may be a major reason for your contacts not coming into the business or dropping out in the early stages

3. *Check with your guest the day before* to make sure they are still coming. Guests who 'no show' are one of the Pigs Around The Corner. The best way to avoid this is to collect the guest from their home

4. *The required dress code is business wear.* Do not be surprised if you or your guest are turned away at the door for not wearing business dress, so advise your guests of the dress code

5. *Get there early.* You may find the doors locked against you if you arrive late. Advise your guests that this is a business meeting and will start promptly on time

6. *Set the scene* (the 'C' of playing CUPID). Your guests will feel more relaxed, and will concentrate better on the meeting, if they know what is going to happen. So you should explain beforehand what the procedure will be

7. *Set your guest's mind at rest.* One reason why guests 'no show' is because they are frightened of being talked into something or being put under pressure. Make it clear that this is only a presentation and a discussion, and it is not in your interests if people make the wrong decision by coming in

8. *Sit with your guest, not in the bar.* This seems obvious but, to some distributors, it is not! Even if you have no guest, this is not a social night out. Although people

should enjoy themselves (this is, after all, one of the great attractions of network marketing), at the end of the day the purpose is to support the meeting, not the bar

9. *Make confidence-building introductions.* Introduce your guest to other distributors to whom your guest may relate (these are the Compatible Distributors who, to repeat, do not have to be in our group). You can also introduce them to an upline. If another distributor asks you, always be prepared to meet their guest, whether or not they are in your paylines, or even in our group. One day, you may want the same favour in return!

10. *Hosting.* You should also be prepared to host guests for other distributors, *whether they are in our group or not*, if the distributor has good reasons why they cannot look after them. Although it is obviously better for distributors to host their own guests, in the real world it is not always possible to do so. Remember, if you are asked to do this, that you may well need the favour returned in the future!

11. *Guests at BOMs are not fair game for poaching!* It can happen that a distributor is asked to host a guest for someone else, at the end of which the guest wants that distributor to sponsor them. Although it is a bit hard on the guest, the only way to stop abuse of the system is for the host to say, 'No'

12. *Trust* between distributors in the same company, even if they are in different groups, is so vital that, if you find any distributor in your group trying to poach, or if one is reported to you by another group leader, you should immediately get their distributorship terminated. It *never* pays to give people with that attitude a second chance. Keeping them in your group will affect your honest distributors—who, of course, will make up the very great majority of your people. This action needs to be seen to be taken

13. *Help guests who are obviously 'lost'.* Again, these guests are not fair game for poaching. If the host cannot be found (and it can happen that hosts are unavoidably delayed), you should make sure that the guest is properly looked after. As we saw above, the host does not need to be in our group. Remember, again, that *you* may well break down on the way to a meeting or be held up in traffic delays, and so need the same favour in return

14. *Help the speakers.* A speaker cannot be expected to think up new jokes for every BOM and, in any case, the guests will not have heard that speaker before. The speakers are there to help *you* and *your group*, so the least you and your people can do is to laugh at their jokes!

15. *Help the organisers.* If you have no guest, you should always be prepared to help the organisers in any way you can. The times when this is most appreciated can be in setting up and, especially, in packing everything away afterwards

16. *If testimonials are a feature of the BOM*, you should be prepared to give one if asked

17. *Keep quiet—resist asides.* Nothing undermines a speaker more than people apparently not listening. You may be telling your guest what a great person the speaker is, but the speaker won't know that and nor will the other guests; if they see you having a whispered conversation, they will think that you are bored

18. *Wear your badge (if the company supplies them).* Many distributors feel it is embarrassing or a 'bit over the top' to wear badges, but they serve some very useful functions:

 a) Experienced distributors at meetings are always looking to help other distributors and badges help to differentiate guests from distributors

b) Distributors cannot be expected to remember everyone's names

c) A badge tells an experienced distributor your position on the compensation plan and helps them to 'pitch' their conversation in the best way to help you

d) It looks very good to a guest when an experienced distributor saunters over, addresses you by name and apparently knows you well (you, of course, will instantly recognise their senior position and learn their name from their badge)! Little does the guest know that you have never met before—the badges have done it all!

19. *You and your distributors should be ambassadors for yourselves, our group and the company.* As far as a guest is concerned the BOM is the company's showcase, so make sure it is a good one. BOMs are also often a guest's first experience of the *network in action* and we all know how important first impressions are.

(*You can apply many of these guidelines to all events*)

Run great sizzle sessions!

There are a number of considerations which apply specifically to sizzle sessions.

Sizzle sessions are hardly used in some groups and much under-valued in others. Nevertheless, they can be extremely valuable to your business because they are an important way to build team spirit (this is the 'T' for **Team-mindedness** of being a teaching ACTTER) and they help to keep your business structured and motivated down to a very local level.

A group which holds regular, *properly structured* sizzle sessions will be very much stronger than the same group without

---

Many sizzle sessions over time degenerate into an excuse for a weekly or monthly social get-together for the group. Although this will still have some motivational benefit for the group (*anything* which gets members of your business together will help the team-building), very little else of business value results from these meetings.

One answer is to have an agreed structure for sizzle sessions and then, by Constant Repetition, ensure that your group follows this structure so that everyone is running meetings of value.

Sizzle sessions in groups which have not yet generated their own momentum should be held weekly to begin with, on the same day and at the same time so that distributors can plan around them well ahead.

When a group has generated its own momentum and stabilised, the leaders' sizzles often drop to monthly, although newer groups further down in each leg will still be holding weekly sizzles.

A distributor should attend their upline's sizzle session (this is part of the BACTA). They should also hold a sizzle for their own group. As their group grows, they should then attend sizzles being held by distributors downline of them (this target is also included in the BACTA), as part of Working With their people.

A good way to organise a sizzle

First, a quarter of an hour's formal training

The purpose of the formal training section is to remind your distributors of the basics. If people are not constantly reminded of the basics, they start complicating the concept and Go Off-Track. The only way to Stay On-Track is by Constant Repetition, and sizzles are a perfect platform for this. You can take a chapter from one of the books in the S.T.A.R. Leadership Programme as a base for your presentation.

This fifteen minutes of formal training is also an excellent way for your potential speakers to get used to the idea of public speaking and formal training. But fifteen minutes is quite enough; the purpose of a sizzle is not to hold a formal training session.

Second, use the sizzle as a notice board

Sizzle leaders should pass on communications from the company, their uplines and, of course, anything they wish to communicate to their own people.

Make sure sizzle leaders *check for understanding*—in other words, that everyone is clear on what those communications mean.

Third, the rest of the session should be devoted to Reactive Training

This means that the meeting should react to what the distributors need rather than to what the trainer wants. Sizzles are primarily Reactive Training meetings (see page 175).

So both the formal training and the notice board should be despatched as quickly as possible. Then the sizzle leader should throw the meeting open to whatever topics those attending wish to discuss. *It is vital that the leader should keep their own wishes out of the equation at this stage,* which means that those leaders who run the best sizzles are the ones who keep their own egos furthest out of sight!

However, as leader, you should keep everyone to the point under discussion. Also, make sure quieter people are encouraged to speak and to raise topics for discussion, and that the more dominant ones are both kept in check and do not dictate the topics.

Often, when a someone asks me to look into why they are finding it difficult to get people to attend their sizzles, the problem is caused by the leader 'hogging' the limelight, often combined with being impatient of people's views. The fact is, people attending want, and need, to be heard and treated sympathetically and with respect. If the meetings do not allow them to clear the air and deal with the problems which are causing them concern, it is hardly surprising if they do not want to give up their own time to attend.

How to control the quality of the sizzles in your group

If you are Working With an inexperienced distributor who has developed a big enough group to start their own sizzles, you will need to give them some help until they are confident of running them on their own.

Several days prior to the event, discuss with them what formal training would be most valuable for the first fifteen minutes of their sizzle session and then ask *them* to prepare the notes for the presentation because this way they will learn far more than they would if you do it for them. You should then discuss their notes with them to make sure that the content is right.

The formal training should be backed up by a visual. Most fifteen-minute sessions will only need one visual, but some may need two or three depending on the topic. As sizzle sessions by definition should be confined to small groups, an A3 sheet for the visual is normally enough. The alternative is to give each distributor photocopied A4 sheets. Either way, distributors should take away notes to read at home, as part of Constant Repetition, and to pass onto *their* distributors who did not come to the sizzle.

Go as a guest to as many downline sizzle sessions as you can. Although the sizzle leader and his or her distributors will find it great motivation to have you there and that in itself is a great reason for going, *your purpose is not to take the meeting over.*

The reasons for attending sizzle sessions are partly to keep your profile high and partly to Work With your sizzle leaders, helping them to present themselves better (being a better ACTTER), to present their content better (learning to KISS and play CUPID) or to help their people get more out of the sizzle sessions. Agree in advance who will do what, and review the sizzle afterwards with the leader.

In particular, remember to *respect your sizzle leader's sphere of influence* (page 157) by supporting their position. You do this partly by making sure you do not take the meeting over. Confirm their position in the minds of their distributors as much as you can, and thank them in public for having invited you to their meeting. That way, you will build their loyalty and confidence in you and you will always find yourself welcome at their meetings.

Chapter 22

Winning Leaders Control Direction

Winning Leadership = Training +
DIRECTION + Motivation

In this chapter, we are going to look at how you should direct your business.

If your aim is to build a *high-level* business, then:

Direction means having leaders in place capable of duplicating your methods and standards throughout your business

---

Therefore:

As a winning leader, spot the leaders!

In other words, apply the *Keystone Law: How successful you are will depend on how many teachers and leaders you develop in your group.* You should start to look for and develop other winning leaders straightaway.

If you intend to be a big business-builder, your aim is not merely to sponsor distributors, it is to sponsor *leaders*. Having said that, just as you cannot tell beforehand who will, and who will not, succeed as a distributor, you equally *cannot tell beforehand who will, and who will not, succeed as a leader.* Therefore, the only way you will find the leaders you need is by continuing to sponsor distributors. Sponsor enough, and eventually the winning leaders you need will start to emerge.

Given that anyone can become a leader and teacher, let's not overstate what a leader and teacher is. Remembering that *Doing the job **is** teaching it; teaching the job **is** doing it*:

Anyone who will stick to doing the job as it should be done and will teach others to do the same is a leader and teacher

---

That does not sound as if you are asking for much and you are not, so you might expect that leaders would be easy to find. But this is one of The Pigs Around The Corner for a leader because, as the City of Dreams story tells you (Chapter 6, *Get Off To A Winning Start*), although all can make the effort, few will.

What do you look for in a leader?

What you are looking for in a leader is the same as you want in a distributor (page 88) only more of it:

---

1. Do they have a *burning* desire to succeed in network marketing?
2. Do they have an *insatiable Hunger to Learn*
3. Will they *consistently apply* what you teach with *Drive and Focus*?

People with these three qualities bypass the need for talent; the more of these qualities they have, the greater the leaders they will become. People with high levels of these attributes are very hard to find which is why we call them 'Stars', so don't make the mistake of passing them over in favour of other distributors who may initially appear to have more obvious leadership qualities because they present themselves well at the start.

So, when you are looking for your leaders, focus on these three qualities above all else. Just because we are talking about leaders does not mean that you are looking for intelligence, or previous experience, or education, or articulateness or the 'right' background any more than you would with a distributor. Sticking to this principle may mean that you have to spend a lot of extra time teaching someone because they seem to have absolutely nothing going for them *except* a Burning Desire, a Hunger to Learn and a determination to apply what they learn, but:

Would you rather work for six months carving a solid rock into shape for your business, or would you prefer to put less time and effort into moulding putty?

How long should you spend with a trainee leader?

Remember: *Although attitudes (i.e., Drive and Focus) determine how well they **will** act, knowledge determines how well they **can** act.* Therefore,

---

A trainee leader should not be left to get on with it on their own until they are at least as good as you are at teaching and leading their own business

---

If they are not, standards of teaching and leadership will dilute as they travel down your group.

Many groups unaccountably stop growing once they reach a certain size. You will often find that the leaders at the top of the group and those in their immediate sphere of responsibility do the job right but, because they do not have the right leadership training in place, this has gradually diluted as the message has gone down the network.

But if you teach your leaders properly they may well end up *better* than you because you will have taught them everything you know, to which they will graft all their own talents and abilities. Then you will truly enjoy the fruits of your efforts!

Some trainee leaders will have your brains and experience picked clean in a matter of weeks. Others may take six months—it does not matter *because there is no time-limit on creating winning leaders.* Provided they Stay On-Track, stick with them for however long it takes. It is hard enough finding people with these levels of determination without giving up on them because they are slow learners!

How to find and develop 'Stars'

People who want to be active leaders ('top dogs' and 'first lieutenants', see page 35) are very rare. These people are the 'Stars' who will bring sparkle to your business. When you spot one, arrange with their sponsor that you will make them your protégé: someone whose training you will make your special responsibility.

The extra training you should give them is to include them in every meeting and activity you can. Make them your shadows. If they are not present at an activity, involve them in the planning and review it with them afterwards to pick out the lessons.

When you have finished teaching your first 'Star', you should move on to find another while your first 'Star' teaches *their* first. This gives you *four* 'Stars' in your business. The four 'Stars' will each then teach a new one, giving you *eight* 'Stars' in your business.

As you can see, you can make the Geometric Progression work on your 'Star' leadership base just as it should on your distributor base. If it takes an average of four months to train each 'Star', at the end of two years you will have 64 in your business. Even if it takes six months, you will still have 16 'Stars' in your business—with 32 just six months later. In the real world, this will happen much more slowly because you won't find enough people prepared to make the necessary commitment. But I think you can see the point I am making: you need a system to spot the 'Stars', to make them as good as they can be, and to ensure that they do the same with *their* 'Stars'. Sadly, most people squander the potential of their 'Stars' by assuming they have nothing to teach them and leaving them to their own devices.

While your group will grow well without 'Stars' (which is what this Programme is about), each one who does come in will generate explosive expansion for your business. If you use the system I recommend to find and develop them, 'Stars' will increasingly begin to appear in your business, but it will take time. So, in developing their leaders, a winning leader has to have the Patience to give the Geometric Progression time to work.

Direction means Communication

Unless your distributors are kept fully up to-date with all developments and with everything they need to know, they *cannot* do the best possible job for you.

General communications, such as newsletters which go out direct from the company to each distributor, are rarely a complete answer. If winning leaders want to ensure that their distributors are kept fully briefed on activities within their group, they must take on this responsibility themselves.

By reporting on developments and success stories within your group, your own newsletter helps to foster team spirit (the 'T' of being a Teaching ACTTER). By promoting trainings and quality learning materials, it can help foster a Hunger to Learn. And, by using Constant Repetition to drive home the basics of doing the business, your newsletter can help ensure that people are Staying On-Track.

The phone is another excellent way of getting communication through to every distributor. Any good upline will always be looking for excuses to phone their distributors, and having information to pass on is a good excuse!

You can also use the 'notice-board' section at sizzle sessions to get communications to all your distributors.

Direction means that each distributor has a sense of purpose

If people do not know what their destination is, how do they know in which direction to go? They don't—so they stop. A sense of direction, or a sense purpose, call it what you will, is achieved by having personal goals. If people know what their personal goals are, they can be shown in which direction to go. Network marketing is simply a vehicle for people to reach their destination.

People forget their direction in life very easily *unless someone keeps reminding them*. It is up to *you*, a winning leader, to make sure that the need for focusing on personal goals is *continuously* stressed throughout your group as an essential part of achieving success. This is why *Focus on your purpose* and *Focus your actions on success* are included in the Six Winning Attitudes.

Your main tools for achieving this are the Goals Sheet and the BACTA, which is the plan for turning goals into focused actions (Chapter 3, *Get Off To A Winning Start*, and *Target Success!*)

Direction means having a standardised training system throughout your business

This is the main benefit for you of the S.T.A.R. Leadership Programme. If everyone is being taught in the same way, everyone benefits. Perhaps more than anything else, this creates a strong sense of everyone in your group 'pulling in the same direction'. The previous chapters gave you all you need to know to achieve this in your business.

Direction means giving a good example

Being a winning leader means doing everything you did to become a successful network marketeer and a winning teacher—*but doing more of it—and showing other people how to do it!*

> **More than in any other business I know, in network marketing, people take their lead from the top**

Give a good example to your group and you will be giving the strongest possible direction to your leaders and to your distributors.

Leading from the front, lighting the path for other people to follow, is the best example to give.

> **The pace of the pack is determined by the pace of the leader**

So, every night, make it a habit to review the day by asking yourself, *If every one of my people does what I did today, how would my business grow?* Did you really behave like someone leading from the front? Did you really give your people a good example not just in what they did see, but in what they *didn't* see? In other words, are you practising what you preach as a habit, whether people are there or not? Because, if you do not, why should they?

One good example you can give is to *Never forget that you were once a struggling distributor.* So give a helping hand to anyone who asks for it, whether they are in your business or not. If you generously give of your time, knowledge and experience to other people, you will not be a just winning leader, you will be a *great* leader!

Direction means controlling the ethical standards of your group

This was covered in Chapter 14 of *Get Off To A Winning Start*, including a useful Code Of Professional Ethics. Be relentless in your quest to ensure that everyone in your business sticks to the standards you lay down.

Direction means controlling the structure of your business

The reason why such large incomes are available through network marketing is because there is no theoretical limit to the number of frontline people you can develop directly beneath you—unlike conventional organisations, where it is generally excepted that one person can manage *properly* only between five and ten people reporting directly to them.

The reason why one person can successfully manage an open-ended number of people frontline is because the techniques required to be a winning sponsor, retailer, teacher, leader and business-builder are so simple that they can be quickly and easily learnt and taught—*provided the teacher and leader go about it in the right way*. Once taught, they require only Constant Repetition and vigilance to help people to Stay On-Track.

So here is the dilemma: how should you divide your time between sponsoring new people into your own frontline, and Working With leaders and distributors in existing legs of your business?

Control the structure by 'anchoring' each leg

Structure = Security is part of the Six Winning Attitudes because the way you structure your business can make a dramatic difference both to your earnings and to the strength of your group. No matter how good you are at the Four Must-Do Activities and no matter how good a leader you are, if you do not develop the right strategy for building your business, *and if you do not teach your people to do the same*, your earnings will be much lower than they ought to be and your business will be much less solid than it could be.

Each person you take on frontline is creating a new leg for you. Your next aim is to *anchor* that leg, which means developing it to the stage that it no longer needs your day-to-day input because the distributors are perfectly capable of 'growing' that leg with no help from you.

Each leg you establish is in fact a separate business in its own right, and you can compare this with a conventional businessperson who owns many different 'companies'—none of which require their daily input because each has its own experienced management team.

The strategy we talk about here may need to be adapted to make best use of the compensation plan of your company.

There are three basic rules to building a solid business:

1. **Anchor** (also called **Secure** or **Consolidate**) each leg before moving onto the next one

2. Build deep before building wide

3. Teach your people to do the same.

The message is:

1. Limit how many frontlines you start with. In fact you cannot start with too few but you can easily take on too many

How many frontlines you should start with depends on, first, how much time you are devoting to the business and, second, how much time any *frontliner* you are Working With gives to the business. If you are working all hours and the first few people you sponsor are part-time, you could start with as many as five or six but, if you have any doubts at all, err on the side of taking on too few.

If you are *part*-time but you sponsor a *full*-time frontliner, you owe it both to them and to yourself to keep your frontline to one until their business is up and running.

2. Then, do not sponsor anyone else frontline until at least one of your previous frontline legs is anchored

If you move onto a new leg before the one you are leaving is fully anchored, it may well collapse, which means that you have wasted all that time and effort. In this case, all you are achieving by sponsoring frontline is to make up for the legs which are collapsing, instead of sponsoring to expand your business. You have got yourself into a *Sponsoring Sieve* (page 59).

To both avoid this and structure your business properly, adopt the business strategy of *Working Deep, Not Wide*. In other words, work deep down one leg, helping the distributors in that leg, until the leg can support itself.

How can you judge when a leg is anchored?

An anchored leg can also be called 'a self-supporting leg' or, 'a stand-alone leg', but how do you know when you have achieved this and can safely move on to develop a new leg? Here are the two most common approaches, neither of which I recommend:

1. One view is that you can move on and leave a leg to support itself as soon as you have a 'serious' distributor somewhere in that leg capable of showing the business.

Apart from distributors who bring in everyone frontline to themselves and therefore have no strategy at all, this strategy is by far the most frequently used but it has two serious flaws:

> **i)** What happens if that one 'serious' distributor drops out? The leg will collapse

> **ii)** You will have moved to a new leg before that one serious distributor knows as much as you about the business. So the standards of teaching and leadership will drop as they go down the levels as increasingly untrained people retail the product and show the business.

2. According to the second approach, you have anchored the leg once you have 'taught "A" to teach "B" to sponsor "C"', as explained by Don Failla in his book *The Basics*[1].

But the philosophy I would recommend is a third one:

A leg is only anchored when:
1. You have found and taught a downline within the leg who can teach and lead at least as well as you can, *and*
2. The leg is generating its own momentum

If you pass the leadership baton for a leg to a leader who cannot do the job at least as well as you can, this will duplicate down that leg and the quality of tuition and leadership will fall at each level. But, if you teach each leader in each leg not to pass the hands-on responsibility for that leg, until *they* have found and taught a network marketeer to teach and lead *at least as well as they can*, your standards of tuition and leadership will continue right to the bottom level of each leg.

The Principle of Momentum and Momentum Generators

Anchoring a leg also means that you have to take the drop-out rates into account. Drop-out rates vary enormously, but the average seems to be between 75% and 90% per year in a group of any size. On this basis, of the first ten distributors in any one leg, only one or two will stay. Hardly a strong leg!—Yet ten names on a computer print-out looks good and will fool any new distributor into thinking that leg is growing well and that they can move on to sponsor a new frontliner.

Therefore, even if you have an apparently strong leader emerging in that first ten, it might still be too soon to start

---

1. Published by MLM International

a new leg. Because, at the moment, *you* are the person creating momentum (what we call *The Momentum Generator*) in that leg. If you remove your focus from that leg, you could be taking its source of momentum away before your new leader is ready to take over the baton, and the leg may well collapse. It certainly will hesitate in its growth. So you need to continue working in that leg until it has *created its own momentum*, meaning that the new leader is capable of continuing to generate momentum after you have passed them the baton for that leg. In other words, you should create new momentum generators in that leg *before* leaving it not, as is generally the case in the industry, uplines hoping that momentum generators will appear *after* they have stopped working in a leg.

The answer is to drive hard down that leg, Working With any likely looking leaders who emerge, until you have enough distributors in position to anchor the leg.

Don't worry about how many levels down these Momentum Generators are because under the principle of **Compression** they will come up into your paylevels.

Business-building in this way can sound like a drawn-out operation, but it is an illusion caused by impatience and lack of experience that, by building wide, you will build a bigger business more quickly. Once again, the lesson is to be patient and to work methodically. Particularly if you use the All-Out Massive Action Programme, or the Fast Sponsoring methods in Chapter 14 of *Breakthrough Sponsoring & Retailing*, you will achieve a solid base to your business more quickly and, once you have achieved that, business expansion will be both dramatically faster and more solid than with groups where the leaders have tried to cut corners at the start.

In most compensation plans, one of the benefits of a promotion might be that you qualify for royalty payment on an extra generation. For instance, you may start by receiving royalty on three generations but, when you reach a certain position on the compensation plan, your royalties may then be paid on four generations.

This is excellent news, *provided that you actually have four generations to be paid on!* People who have structured their businesses wide rather than deep may find that, when payment on that extra generation 'switches in', they have not built a business deep enough to take advantage of it, whereas someone who has built their business deep in the way we have described, may well find themselves benefiting immediately from payments on the extra generation.

In the example we have just given, you could therefore say that a leg is anchored when you can be sure of four generations of qualifiers in at least one line of the leg—in other words, four serious distributors downline of each other—so that you can take immediate advantage of the benefits of promotion. This may not sound very important until you realise that each level in your business potentially *has more distributors on it than **all** the levels above **added together**!* Looked at in this way, it is not inconceivable that your income will double overnight each time you qualify for an extra generation for payment.

So another definition of an anchored leg is:

---

1. You have found and taught a network marketeer in the leg who can teach and lead *at least as well as you can*, and
2. In at least one line in that leg, you are taking advantage of all your generations for payment

---

How does building wide differ from building deep?

Let's assume that you, personally, rush out and sponsor 30 people. If you build a frontline as wide as you can and therefore put all 30 people frontline to yourself, your business would look like the diagram below (we'll call this model 'A').

Model 'A': Building Wide

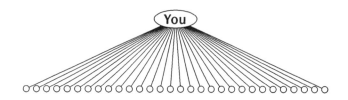

I hasten to add that this is not duplicatable because it takes an exceptional recruiter to sponsor 30 people off their own contact list or through cold market efforts! And we have, of course, ignored any sponsoring done by your people; this is only a simplified model for demonstration purposes. But you can already see the problem: how can you possibly give proper support to 30 new and inexperienced people reporting directly to you? And, if you have not taught them properly, what sort of support will they give to their people?

Contrast that with 30 distributors sponsored into your business, but this time in a business built deep (we'll call this model 'B').

As you can see, in model 'B' you built a frontline team of only three people and, also as you can see, you have taught your people to do the same. This makes the job of managing your business very much easier than it was in model 'A', because you are now only having to deal directly with three people (although you will be helping them to teach some of their people) and asking them to duplicate the same approach downwards.

Your first line (to the extreme left) has already gone down seven levels—which means that the last distributor in that line has *six* people above them, all of whom are available to help them to build their business.

Model 'B': Building Deep

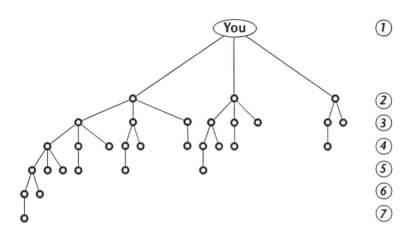

So these models hide the fact that your distributors in model 'B' will have stayed in the business longer and sponsored many more people than they would have done in model 'A' because of the very much greater level of upline support available to each distributor.

Model 'B' also means that you are already getting well into your royalty paylevels, with a base already growing to take immediate advantage of any additional paylevels which come with promotion.

Now let's look at the level of support your people are getting

In model 'B', there are only three people (your frontline) who have only one upline (you) to call on for help. Of the rest, eight have two uplines to help; ten have three uplines to help; six have four uplines to help; two have five uplines to help and one has six uplines to help. Contrast this with 'A' where all 30 have only one upline (you) to help them. An impossible task! Is 'B' not the much stronger business?

This level of support helps to limit drop-outs, adding further impetus to the dramatically accelerated business growth which is the result of intensive upline support.

Because of the lack of support each distributor gets, model 'A' can only possibly work if you recruit people who are capable of getting results on their own. This presents two severe problems to those who have tried it—and many have, the classic idea being to concentrate on recruiting trained salespeople. First, as only, say, 2% of the population can operate with this lack of support, you have cut the available market for distributors from nearly 100% of people who, with the right support, are capable of being successful distributors to the 2% who have the ability to succeed without proper training. Network marketing is for all, and you have broken that rule. Second, if you target trained salespeople, there are nowhere near enough to go round.

People who try to build businesses in this way stack the cards heavily against themselves, and I hope you can see why.

Finally, model 'B' is very much less wasteful of both your Contact List and the Contact Lists of your people because you (as does each distributor) spend more time helping other distributors work their Contact Lists, and correspondingly less time working on your own. This has the added benefit that, when you do go back to work your list, it is with greatly increased confidence because:

One of the most compelling sponsoring aids is that you have helped a downline to build a successful business, giving yourself and others the confidence that you can help someone else to do the same

---

But this means that you have got to create a success story first and the sooner you do that, by concentrating on one leg, the better.

Have you any doubts that, had you built your business deep by following model 'B', things would already be looking good whereas, had you built it wide according to model 'A', you could still be struggling?

I once met a distributor who, through an astonishing recruiting effort, brought in 280 people frontline. Three months later, only two legs remained active; one month later, he was down to one! Although this is an extreme instance, you will find many less dramatic examples of the folly of building wide rather than deep.

Now, to round off the S.T.A.R. Leadership Programme, we turn to the problem of how you, as a winning leader, can motivate your people to do what it takes to succeed.

Chapter 23

It's Easy To Be A Great Motivator!

Winning Leadership = Training + Direction
+ **MOTIVATION**

We have looked closely at training and direction; now we will look at how to be a successful motivator.

This is, perhaps, the aspect of leadership which worries people most. They think that a great motivator must be a larger than life character with a powerful, magnetic personality and lots of charisma. They think that they must be able to get up on stage and raise the hearts and minds of people with gifted oratory. And they think they have none of these gifts. The odds are that you, reading this, are probably right—you probably do have none of these gifts! *But that does not mean you cannot become a winning motivator, able to build a large, successful business.*

If you are not a larger than life character, you can replace this with conviction and certainty (the 'C' of being an ACTTER) in what you are doing, the ability to communicate that to other people, the willingness to learn and apply the techniques we have talked about in the S.T.A.R. Leadership Programme, and a single-minded determination to reach your goals.

This is something anyone can do. It depends only on how much they want to and what action they are prepared to take to make it happen. By the time you finish this chapter, you should feel comfortable that there is nothing here you could not do.

What is motivation?

Motivation is a concept rarely understood by conventional managers. They see it as something they impose on other people and it is often defined as the 'carrot and the stick' principle. Carrots are pay rises, promotions, the trappings of status and a whole variety of incentive schemes, competitions and bonuses. Sticks are fear of losing one's job, missing pay rises and promotions, being shown up in front of one's work-mates or incurring the wrath of superiors.

You can see that there is a lot of bribery and fear-mongering in this. But none of this is real motivation.

Real, ongoing motivation consists of four things:

1. People *wanting* to work for their boss and their company, not *having* to

2. People working for what *they* want, not for what the company wants out of them

3. People knowing what they want to achieve in life

4. People seeing how they can achieve their goals through working in your business.

What conventional business calls motivation is *short-term* in its effect and depends mainly on either offering material gain or status, or threatening their loss. These are hardly noble appeals to the emotions!

The motivation we are talking about is based on *people* values: people working because they want to work for a particular individual and people working for what they want to achieve for themselves, not for what the company wants out of them. If people work for you because they want to, that is long-term motivation. If people see how they can achieve their goals in life through working in your business, that, too, is long-term motivation.

I will show you how to truly motivate your people long-term. Let me just rephrase what I said above, because it is so important:

Long-term motivation means motivation from *within* the person being led (*self-motivation*), not motivation imposed from outside by the leader

---

The way to make people want to work for you is to earn their loyalty

Loyalty is not a right, it is an *earned* privilege. Traditional managers would have you believe that, because they are senior to you, they are *entitled* to expect your loyalty and because a company or organisation pays you a salary or wage, it has the right to your loyalty. Both of these beliefs are wrong and contribute to the appalling state of British business and institutions. A company which thinks that it is entitled to your loyalty merely because it pays you an income has not *earned* your loyalty, it is trying to buy it. If you sell your loyalty on those terms, you risk selling your soul.

Employees, too, either individually or through their trade unions, now believe that they have rights to income and employment without the responsibility of giving value back to the company, the organisation or society. This, of course, stems from the example they have received from their employers.

In a healthy environment, a company or organisation should expect that it must *earn* your loyalty by respecting and treating you properly—then, of course, it is entitled to it.

In a healthy environment, managers know that they are entitled to an employee's loyalty only if they take steps to *earn* it—then, of course, they are entitled to expect it. That way, managers know that they must work very hard at being good managers of people.

In a healthy environment, employees know that they are entitled to the loyalty of their company and managers only in return for quality work and good productivity—then, of course, they are entitled to it.

I have gone into this in some detail because you will find many people who come into your business expecting support from you (in other words, your loyalty) but only expecting to do the minimum in return. They expect you to build their business for them. They expect you to run training sessions for the group at week-ends (which is the best time to run trainings) but they can have the week-end off. They expect you to host a guest at a BOM or do a One-to-One for them because they want to socialise. They feel that a dinner invitation is a good enough reason to miss your regular Tuesday evening sizzle. In other words, they feel they have rights without responsibilities.

You will also find group leaders who feel that their position entitles them to the loyalty of their group without them having done anything to earn it.

Loyalty is a two-way contract

As a winning leader, you must expect that you are only entitled to loyalty if you *earn* it.

The only true way network marketing leaders can earn the loyalty of their distributors is by getting out there and *Working With* them

---

The more you do that, the more loyalty you will earn and the more loyalty you can expect in return.

> The only true, worthwhile loyalty a distributor can give you is to repay your efforts on their behalf by their efforts on your behalf

... such efforts, of course, being just as much to their own benefit!

Of course, on day one, a new distributor has not yet had a chance to do anything to earn your loyalty. So, in the first instance, they deserve *all* your loyalty as of right.

But, thereafter, you are looking for as much loyalty back in terms of them doing the tasks they agree to do, to the best of their ability.

> Whether they do their tasks well or badly does not matter, it is the actions and the attitude behind them that matter: did they do what they agreed, and did they do it as well as they could?

If the answer is 'No', leave that distributor to their own devices because they no longer merit your loyalty. If you continue to Work With them, you are merely making them *Dependent* on you; you are also giving a bad example to your people which will, according to the Theory of Duplication, spread throughout your group. Find instead another new distributor or give your loyalty to those distributors who are repaying your loyalty with their own.

Earn loyalty by learning to love your people!

Love is the great motivator. Think of the people in your life who matter most to you; it could be your parents, your spouse or loved one, your children. It could be brothers or sisters. Of all these people, you can say publicly that you 'love' them. But we also love many other people in our lives: great friends, close colleagues, caring teachers, spiritual leaders, a mentor who has guided us, faithful employees or (if we are lucky!) a 'boss' who really helped us.

These are the people in your life for whom you will do the most. For some, you would be prepared to give your life. What has motivated you to show such loyalty to them? Love. If other people can generate that motivation in you through love, you can use the same power to motivate others.

To be a power, love must be shown. If it is not, it might as well not exist; it has no value. If you want to make it mean most to the recipient, show it in the way the recipient most wants it to be shown. In the case of your people, they value your love most in the way you *appreciate* them, show *pride* in them, *praise* them, *care* for them and for what you *do* for them.

Show **Appreciation** for what people do for you and they will work harder, more willingly and more happily for you.

Show **Pride** in people and they will feel pride in themselves. A group which shows pride in itself is a very strong group! Pride is a massive motivating power and one of the Six Winning Attitudes.

Giving **Praise** shows both love and appreciation. Look for opportunities to appreciate people's efforts and praise them. When you have to criticise, balance this with appreciation for the effort they are making on your behalf and praise for what they do well.

At meetings or in newsletters, pick out people to compliment. But not just the obvious high-flyers; in any group the vast majority of your people will be part-timers, often looking only for a small income from network marketing. They, too, deserve to be appreciated. It is not motivating for them if the only people ever chosen for mention are the high-flyers. If you use incentive schemes, make sure that part-timers and small business-builders can also win something.

Show you **Care** about your people, and care about them you should because *you* will get nowhere without their efforts! Even in a business of thousands of people, each one is a special person in their own right.

One drop of rain achieves nothing but enough drops of rain will cause a mighty flood. One distributor may earn you little but enough of them will solve your ATAC equation!

Going to as many meetings as possible, circulating among your people and having a few encouraging words with as many people as possible shows how much you care.

Distributors in any group split into two: those with established businesses and those without established businesses. Distributors with established businesses can get into the comfort zone of spending too much time with each other but it is not each other you need—you are already successful people. You can only keep your success going by continuously applying the Keystone Law and making *new* people successful—in other words, by continuously helping other distributors to get their businesses established. So you should spend *as little time as possible* with each other and *as much time as possible* with distributors without established businesses.

At trainings, meetings, business or social events, those with established businesses should make a point of not sitting or grouping together, but of being well spread among those who do not yet have established businesses. The only exception might be speakers at a formal training; they are often best seated at the back, leaving the front rows for those who matter—the trainees. If you are used to conventional business, mixing with other ranks might not be the way you were taught to behave as a manager but, in our business, it pays to show your people that you care enough to seek them out and want to spend time with them.

> If you make sure your people feel the better for you passing by, and if you teach your leaders to do the same, then you truly care for your people and they will care for you

Leaders in traditional business and institutions are appallingly bad at making people feel appreciated for their efforts and praised for their good work; and when did you last hear of a manager in conventional business who really cared for their people or was proud of them? Yet:

> Nothing else earns as much loyalty. Nothing else so easily turns a winning leader into a great leader

Showing people that you will work hard for them earns their loyalty

If people can see that you will 'pull out all the stops' for them, the good ones among them will do the same for you. Working With and lots of it, making them aware that yours is an ever-open door, an ever-ready phone, an ever-listening ear and that nothing is too much trouble, are all ways of showing that you will work hard for them.

But, as I have said many times, you should not work harder for them than they are prepared to work for themselves. There is a fine dividing line here but an important one because, once people become Dependent on you, they *will no longer be loyal to you*; they will simply take you for granted and expect you to do things for them.

> Too many leaders have found out to their
> cost that you can do too much for people
> *who are not doing enough for themselves*

To your amazement, these people will not there for *you*
when you need them.

Making people realise that their success matters to you, earns their loyalty

This is another way of applying the Keystone Law. You
should be more concerned about the success of your people than you are about your own success. If people feel that
you are helping them for themselves, you will build loyalty. If they believe that you are only helping them to help
yourself, their loyalty to you will be limited by their own
self-interest; in other words, they will be using you in the
same way as you are using them. It sounds like a contradic-
tion, but it is true:

> If you care more about other people's
> success than about your own, you will
> actually be *more* successful—and happier

Would you rather look back on life and congratulate yourself on how successful you have been, or would you rather
look back and congratulate yourself on how many other
people have become successful through your efforts? The
latter will make you more successful both in your own eyes
and in the eyes of others.

The way to earn the greatest loyalty is to become a mentor!

Outside immediate family and love relationships, people
give their greatest loyalty to a mentor. If it is the mentors

who generate the strongest feelings of loyalty, does it not make sense for *you* to become the mentor of your group?

The dictionary defines a mentor as, 'A wise or trusted adviser or guide.' The ACTTER Formula shows you exactly how to become trusted by your group and the best way to become a winning teacher and leader is to become an adviser or guide in business terms.

But a mentor goes much further than that. A mentor becomes a 'wise and trusted adviser or guide' in *all* aspects of a person's life, whether business or private.

Network marketing, more than almost any other business, has very blurred dividing lines between business and private life—in fact, the two soon become inseparably linked. This is caused partly by the nature of the business which is person-to-person in the home, partly by the involvement of the family in business matters, whether they are officially signed up or not, and partly because there is not the separation of time between business and personal life which you get in most jobs.

A distributor's quality of work is also directly affected, especially in the case of a new distributor, by the quality of their private life in a way which happens in few other occupations. This gives a mentor an important part to play in the health of a group.

Mentors have gone out of fashion, partly because of the breakdown of the family unit (mentors were often elders of the family), partly because we no longer respect the wisdom of our elders, and partly because value is no longer placed on practical experience.

You may be confused as to the difference between a mentor and similar roles played by teachers and leaders.

In the final analysis, a teacher or leader is there for the business; a mentor is there for the distributor

---

The two things are not contradictory. Network marketing is a people business: in the long run you will prosper by putting your people's interests before your own short-term concerns. Becoming a mentor, because of the way it deepens and cements relationships, turns a winning leader into a great leader.

So how do you become a mentor?

- Accept that you cannot make anyone choose you as their mentor; the choice rests entirely with them, not with you. They will only do so when:

  i) They have learnt to trust both you and your judgement, *and*

  ii) They realise that you will put them and their interests before those of you and your business

- This sounds like a lengthy process: in fact, if you approach people right, you can have them voluntarily coming to you for advice within minutes of meeting you. The process of helping people to find their goals, involving as it does very intimate discussions of a person's innermost feelings and desires, also gives you a chance to create a mentoring relationship very quickly

- You must, quite genuinely, give them the right advice even if it is not in the immediate interests of you or your business. Once you recognise that the trust this creates between you and your people will add dramatically to your business interests overall, even if in the occasional individual case it does not, this becomes easy to do

- Become a wise person, able to give wise advice. Wisdom is no longer a respected attribute, yet it is vital to being a good mentor. There is no mystique to being wise. Anyone who follows these guidelines will be a wise person:

  – Listen hard and *fully understand* what the problem is and how the person *really feels* about it (not how they ought to feel) *before* giving any advice

  – Give advice not from the standpoint of what you believe, but from the standpoint of what that person needs

– You do this by keeping yourself out of the equation, ignoring your beliefs and attitudes and taking on their beliefs and attitudes

– Be non-judgmental. Show pride in your protégé

– Respect the views of those who think differently to you, no matter how strong your views on that matter

– Accept that is sheer arrogance to assume that your views must be right and that all others who think differently are wrong

– Listen and *learn* from others. Truly wise people have humility in that they know everyone, no matter how young, naive or inexperienced, can teach them something. *Every situation is a learning situation if you let it be so*

– Give respect to everyone and everything

– Keep the emotions out of a discussion so that the real cause of a problem can be found and the best answer sought

– Make time for those people who need your time.

In order to avoid a situation of Dependency, choose to help only those who are making best efforts to help themselves, and make it clear that this is their side of the bargain. This may sound harsh but, in fact, you will be doing the best thing for them. If you let people become Dependent on you, you will do them more harm than good. The finest gift you can give to anyone is to teach them how to stand on their own two feet and learn how to meet life on their terms.

Becoming a mentor is one of the most rewarding things there is in life. It sets up a very special relationship which transcends normal business relationships. But it imposes on you a responsibility to advise at all times in the interests of those you are advising.

The greatest form of motivation is self-motivation

We have seen how to develop self-motivation in people by making them *want* to work for you, by earning their loyalty. Now let's look at the other ways to create *long-term* motivation through *self*-motivation, which we defined as your distributors:

- Working for what they want, not for what you want out of them
- Knowing what they want from life
- Seeing how to achieve what they want by working in your business.

Working for what they want, not for what you want out of them

If people are working for what *they* want, not for what you want out of them, they are with you because they want to be, not because they need to be—obviously a much more self-motivating position to be in!

It is very easy to achieve this: all the way through, I have been saying, *Don't impose your aspirations on your people*—in other words, *Let them choose their aspirations for themselves.*

But, as we discussed earlier, people's aspirations do change, so it is important to keep asking the question: *What are you looking for from the business?*

Help people to find out what they want to achieve in life

It is all very well you letting people choose their own aspirations for their businesses, but it only works if people have aspirations of their own to put there! Too often, people have become rudderless through years of following the aspirations of others; when those are removed, they no longer have their own to put in place. Until they do, they will remain rudderless and not much use to you. Look at what can happen to parents when their children leave home, or to people when they retire.

Employed people can become so used to responding to employers ruling their working lives that they find it very difficult when they have to replace that with self-imposed disciplines. The reason is the same—they have not yet got clear in their own minds the goals worth working for.

Few people are self-motivated, because the things they truly want for themselves have disappeared under a mountain of unwanted 'baggage' which they have steadily accumulated throughout their lives. Self-motivation starts to come alive, and is only possible, when a distributor learns to throw away all that unwanted baggage and to focus on only those things they truly want for themselves.

This is why we place so much emphasis on teaching people to set personal goals.

The single greatest thing you can do to create success for yourself is to find *crystal clear* personal goals which *really* excite you

---

Then, do the job right.

The best way you, as a winning leader, can apply the Keystone Law is to help your people to find *crystal clear* personal goals which *really* excite them

---

Then, show *them* how to do the job right.

But your job does not stop there. It may seem illogical that people should forget about the things they *really* want for themselves, but they do! That unwanted baggage, given half a chance, soon starts to accumulate again! So you should constantly remind your people to use their Goals Sheet and *Focus on their purposes.*

Show people how they can achieve their goals through working in your business

Once a distributor believes an action is a 'must', they will do it.

> If people believe that working in your
> business is the way to get what *they* want
> in life, how much will *you* have to
> motivate them?

It is no good to you that people know what they want to
achieve in life, unless they believe that they can achieve
these things *through your business*. The Goal-to-Goal Ladder
(page 118) shows you exactly how this process works.

You therefore have to give your people the confidence that
network marketing, your company, your product and,
most important of all, *your leadership* are the right vehicle
for them to achieve their ambitions.

Motivate by getting rid of demotivation

Doubts, worries, fears and lack of belief are the biggest barriers to success, and to motivation. There is not room in a
person for both motivation and doubt. A person cannot
reach their highest levels of motivation until all their
doubts have gone. Doubts are like obstacles which fall into
a channel of water—they disrupt its progress, whereas what
you want and they need is a clear channel allowing an
uninterrupted flow of water.

> Even a small doubt can significantly affect
> a person's ability to succeed; like a small
> branch that falls into a river, it can soon
> start to collect other debris around it,
> having an ever-increasing effect on the
> free-flow of the water

The worst thing you can do as a winning leader is to add to
those worries! That does not mean that you should bury
your head in the sand. If a problem is there, it is there. But

contrast these ways in which two leaders dealt with the same problem:

- One came in with a long face and said, 'We have a problem. I want you all to see if you can find an answer to it'

- The other came in with a jaunty air and said, 'I think we have a temporary hiccup here! I want each of you to come up with ways round it and then we'll discuss who has the best solution.'

The first focused the group on the problem, the second on the solution. Accept any problem as being only a temporary deviation and, in public, always show complete confidence in success. If you do not, why should your people?

Share your worries only with your mentor (yes, you too should have one!), with trusted downline leaders whom you know will react positively to the situation and with uplines whose judgement you trust. Apart from that, keep your worries where they belong, shut away in your private office.

Personal development—the greatest weapon at your disposal

At the heart of personal development is one of the Four Must-Do Activities For Success—developing Winning Attitudes.

Your people need to believe in *themselves*. They know that other people can succeed in your business, but can *they?* Do they believe that they have the ability to succeed in your business to the level they need to realise their ambitions? This is where personal development comes in; it teaches them, first, that they *can* achieve and second, *how* to achieve whatever they want in life.

The greatest means you have at your disposal to make yourself as successful as you can be is undoubtedly the power of your mind. The greatest instrument at your disposal to make your *business* as successful as it can be is undoubtedly the collective power of the minds of your distributors.

Look again at the Goal-to-Goal Ladder on page 118, and you will see that of the four steps, *three are all in the mind.* Look again at the S.T.A.R. Success Pyramid (page 64) and you will see that of the five levels, *four are in the mind—and at least half the fifth!*

The massive power of the human mind is refined and focused through the exercise of personal development.

No longer do sportspeople think that they can reach the top of their sport without the practise of personal development. They accept that attitude is more important to winning than natural ability or the amount of training done—important though those are.

Yet those of us from conventional organisations so often dismiss personal development as something 'a bit New Age', perhaps showing a weakness of moral fibre. In conventional business, if you practise it, you certainly do not admit it!

You cannot retain that belief in network marketing. Nearly all the many winning leaders I have met in our industry are great champions and promoters of personal development. Very often, this is because their own great achievements came through practising it.

Network Marketing is often called '*the* personal development business' because the one thing which really matters is having the right attitudes. *You* may have attitudes which do not require the practise of personal development to succeed but, I promise you, most of the distributors in your group will not. But you can show them how to acquire them.

We have spoken often about attitude. *The only way to develop the right attitude is through the exercise of personal development;* there is *no* other way! Whether by accident or design, anyone who has changed their attitudes for the better has already practised personal development.

People can only succeed to the limit of their current capabilities. If their business stops growing, it may be that the answer for them is to increase their current ability through personal development, not seek ways to expand their business.

So, to become a winning leader in network marketing, you will have to:

• Become an expert on personal development (which is not difficult)

• Make its promotion an integral part of the training and leadership policy throughout your business

• Constantly encourage your people to use it.

Although I have covered in depth everything else you need to know to become a winning teacher and leader in network marketing, it is impossible to cover the subject of personal development properly for you here. That needs, and has been given, a book to itself, *Network Marketeers... Supercharge Yourself!* If you have taken my advice, you will have already read and be benefiting from this and other good books on the subject.

Sadly, there are also some dreadful books on personal development so I would ask you to take advice on what books you should get. If you have a book distributor in your network, you can order these through them.

And finally, my best wishes to you all...

Our discussion on motivation brings us to the end of this book and of the S.T.A.R. Leadership Programme. If you put into practise everything we have talked about and lead by example with passion and conviction, I promise you that, whether you have a powerful, charismatic personality or not, whether you consider yourself a natural leader or not, you **WILL** build a highly motivated network of leaders and distributors who will be positively *buzzing!* You, too, can join that elite band of great network marketeers at the top of this fine profession, the one profession which is truly there for all.

You will be quite different from Motivator Michael whom we spoke to in Chapter 3. *He* motivated by pouring high-octane petrol into people's tanks without making any effort to tune their engines or caring enough to see if their engines would take it. *You* will have done it by providing each engine with a qualified and experienced engine-tuner. Motivator Michael might be the all-out, charismatic, fol-low-me-chaps-into-the-jaws-of-hell leader, *but who will fin-ish up with the stronger, more powerful business, you or he?*

I hope that those of you who have a burning desire to become winning leaders, but were wondering if you have the ability, have found reassurance in these pages that you *can* make it...

... That those of you who know you have the talent but could not work out why you were not being as successful as you had expected, have found the answer here...

... And, lastly, that all teachers and leaders, no matter how big or small their businesses, have found here some tips to help them make even more people even more successful.

If so, my efforts will have been repaid manyfold.

I wish for all of you that the wonderful business of network marketing may be the solution to your particular ATAC Equation and open the way to the lifestyle you have cho-sen. And may you, as a winning teacher and a leader, have the enormous satisfaction of helping many others to solve *their* ATAC Equations.

> *'Give me your determination, give me your action, give me your willingness to learn, and I will show you the way.'*

Give to your people the commitment which I gave to you at the start of this book, and you *will* be a winning teacher and leader.

Keep giving value, keep making people feel the better for you passing by, and you *will* be a winning human being

---

Than that, there is no finer accolade.

And may your God or good fortune go with you in your endeavours in life.

(David Barber)

GOVERNMENT HEALTH WARNING!

Knowledge Can Damage Your Health!

Knowledge is not a substitute for getting on and doing it!

If you use training as an excuse for not getting out and DOING, then you have missed the whole point of the S.T.A.R. Leadership Programme!

Glossary

Terms used by the S.T.A.R. Leadership Programme

Any term in *italics* is defined elsewhere in this Glossary.

ACTTER Formula. How to present oneself as a distributor, as a teacher or as a leader, depending on the circumstances:

- Accountability. Be responsible for helping contacts or customers make the right decision for themselves; be responsible for showing and helping distributors to answer their *ATAC Equations*.

- Conviction & Certainty - how you must always appear to potential distributors, distributors in your group, and customers.

- Tell, not Sell when presenting to potential distributors and customers (for teachers and leaders, this becomes Team-mindedness. Make all your people feel part of your team).

- Truth = Trust.

- Enjoyment.

- Respect.

All-Out Massive Action Programme. The ultimate business-building strategy and the ultimate in *Working With*.

Arm's Length Training. Training spent telling distributors what to do, rather than showing them on the job (see *Working With*).

ATAC Equation. Abundant Time, Abundant Cash. Each person's ideal lifestyle. The ATAC Equation is so-called because you can only solve it by ATTACKING the things in life which get in the way of it.

BACTA. See *Business Activity Agreement.*

Balloon Business. A large business built on poor foundations, in contrast to a *Cannonball Business*, which is a large, solid business.

BOM. See *Business Opportunity Meeting.*

Breakaway Group. In many networks, distributors' groups often 'breakaway' from their upline groups once they reach a fixed position on the compensation plan. This does not mean that they become '*Top Dogs*', unless, of course, they want to. Most do not, continuing to co-operate with their uplines on trainings, BOMs, events and day-to-day running.

Bulldozer Mentality. One of the Six Winning Attitudes, made up of two elements: Drive and Urgency In Action. Drive is what creates a Bulldozer Mentality; Urgency In Action is how you express it.

Business Activity Agreement (or BACTA). An agreement made by a distributor with themselves to carry out all those activities which history has proved are essential to success.

Business Opportunity Meeting (or BOM). Variously called Showcase, Business Presentation, Briefing and many other names. A regular presentation (preferably weekly) of the business by experienced distributors for the guests of other distributors.

Cannonball Business. A large, solidly built business, in contrast to a *Balloon Business*, which is a large business built on poor foundations.

Chicken List. The people whom a distributor is embarrassed or frightened to show the business to. Everyone has a Chicken List. Because they are, by definition, those to whom the distributor is closest to or most in awe of, they are the 'hottest' part of anyone's Contact List.

Compatible Distributor. One to whom another distributor can relate because they have something in common such as the same background, occupation, ethnic group, age or sex, or have had to overcome the same problem.

Compression, The Principle Of. When distributors are paid on *Generations* as opposed to levels, each generation (which may consist of many levels) is compressed into one level for the purposes of royalty payments.

Constant Repetition. This is essential to ensure that both distributors and leaders and teachers *Stay On-Track* and avoid complicating the business. It is also essential for teaching slow learners and people who lack business experience.

CUPID Formula. How to apply the *KISS Formula*:

- **C**larify the agenda
- **U**nfolding Step (of the *GUIDE Sequence*): explain benefits, not facts
- **P**atience. Deal with one topic at a time. Unfold at their speed, not yours. Unfold in bite-sized chunks
- **I**nvestigation Step (of the *GUIDE Sequence*): explaining '*Why*' makes people sign up; explaining '*How*' does not
- **D**emonstrate with visual aids.

While CUPID applies to sponsoring, only C, P and D applies to teaching and leading.

Figure-of-Eight Attitude. You are the focal point of the figure '8'. Above are your uplines, below are your downlines. You are the point of communication both ways (see diagram on page 14).

'First Lieutenants'. People who want to be part of the decision-making process of the group, but do not want to run it (see '*Top Dog*'). Akin to directors in conventional business, but who do not want to be managing director. Often big business-builders in their own right.

Formal Trainings. *Arm's Length Trainings* which follow an agenda set by the trainer(s), as opposed to *Reactive Trainings.*

Four Must-Do Activities For Success. The essential activities of Sponsoring, Retailing, Teaching and Applying The *Six Winning Attitudes* which drive them, and which are driven in turn by the Keystone Law (see diagram on page 20). The S.T.A.R. Leadership Programme stands for **S**ponsoring, **T**eaching, **A**ttitudes, **R**etailing.

Generation. A system of calculating royalty payments. Payment by levels often leaves uplines with virtually no royalty income, due to the 75% to 90% inactive rate of distributors in any given month. To boost income, the company includes only qualifiers (i.e. active distributors who have turned over more than a pre-set monthly qualification figure) as counting towards upline royalties (see also *Compression*).

Goals Sheet. An inspiring summary of the most important, burning ambitions you aim to achieve through your business. To be referred to as often as possible, to feel that you have achieved your goals already and to keep yourself focused on your purposes.

Going Off-Track. Missing any one of the elements of *Staying On-Track.*

GUIDE Sequence. The Steps of the Sponsoring Process:

- **G**et-Active Step
- **U**nfolding Step
- **I**nvestigation Step
- **D**ecision Step
- **E**nsuing Step.

Keystone Law. Where training and leadership are concerned: *How successful you become will depend on how many trained leaders and teachers you develop in your group.*

KISS Formula. Keep It Simple and Standard. How to present the business and training (in the latter case, sometimes **K**eep **I**t **S**imple and *Straightforward* applies better). How the KISS Formula is applied is covered by the *CUPID Formula.*

'Lone Wolf'. A distributor who insists on 'doing their own thing', usually refusing to co-operate with uplines.

Momentum Generator. A distributor applying the principles of motivation.

'Pigs Around The Corner'. Problems faced by *all* new teachers and leaders, who should therefore be warned about them.

Reactive Trainings. *Arm's Length Trainings* which react to the group's needs, as opposed to *Formal Trainings.*

Showcase. See *Business Opportunity Meeting.*

Six Planning Commitments. Ideally, these are the commitments you should seek from any new distributor before agreeing to *Work With* them:

1. Commitment to what they want from the business

2. Commitment to your teaching strategy

3. Commitment to their *Business Activity Agreement*

4. Commitment to putting what they learn into practice

5. Commitment to learning

6. Commitment to doing a proper Contact List.

Six Winning Attitudes. One of the *Four Must-Do Activities* which drives the other three: Sponsoring, Retailing and Teaching. The six attitudes are: Be Patient; Have Drive; Be Hungry To Learn; Have Focus; Have Pride; People Buy People.

Sizzle Sessions. Small, regular meetings designed to help and motivate distributors. The agenda should react to their needs and the topics discussed, by and large, should be those chosen by the group.

Sponsoring Sieve. The point at which new distributors being 'poured in' at the top of the 'sieve' only balance those falling out as inactive at the bottom of the sieve; thus the group has effectively stopped growing.

Stacking. Generally, a sponsor puts new distributors into their own frontline. They may, however, give or 'stack' them in a downline distributor's frontline, instead. The downline distributor will now be designated the official sponsor.

'Star'. One of the rare breed of charismatic, natural leaders. It is estimated that only about one in two thousand distributors fall into this category. The purpose of the S.T.A.R. Leadership Programme is to show the other 1,999 people how to succeed as big business-builders.

S.T.A.R. Success Pyramid. The stages of achievement through which every successful person in any field of human endeavour has to go. A useful trouble-shooting tool to isolate where problems in a person's performance might lie.

Staying On-Track. Putting in the time promised; willing to *Work With* and learn from their uplines; and willing to apply what they have learnt with the right attitudes, particularly Drive and Focus.

Steps Of Training. The steps which should be taken in every training assignment.

Explain:
- *What* to do
- *Why* do it and
- *Why* do it that way.

Show:
- *How* to do it.

Check:
- *Check* they understand (i.e. test absorption)
- Then *check* that it is working (i.e. check effectiveness).

Thirty-Minutes-A-Day Habit. Thirty minutes a day spent studying tapes, books and videos. Fifteen minutes should be spent on recapping, fifteen minutes on new study.

'Top Dog'. A big business-builder or top leader who also wants to run their own group. Akin to the managing director of conventional business (see *'First Lieutenants'*).

Training LLAWR. The sources of knowledge: **L**isten to successful distributors; **L**isten to tapes; **A**ttend meetings; **W**atch videos; **R**ead books.

Working With. Giving hands-on help in the field to everyone who is *Staying On-Track*.

More books by David Barber...

Are you missing out on these two companion books to the S.T.A.R. Leadership Programme?

Network Marketeers—Supercharge Yourself! (£8.99)

Now, at last, there is a book about personal development written specifically for network marketeers. Here you will find clear and honest guidance about what personal development can do for you, and how you can apply it to your business.

This is personal development made easy: a straightforward, common-sense approach that anyone can follow.

Personal development is not a cure-all. But if you learn to apply and teach the simple ideas in this book you will supercharge your business and be amazed at how much more rewarding your life will become.

Network Marketeers—Target Success! (£9.99)

Top distributors know that a proper approach to planning your business is the easiest, most sure-fire way to improve your earnings from network marketing.

But where can you find a duplicatable, effective approach that people will really use?

Now David Barber is sharing a proven, easy-to-use system that will meet all your planning needs, including goal-setting, starting off new distributors, the Contact List, personal action planning, managing group growth and keeping track of your money. Give this system a try—the results will delight you!

A prospecting tool you can't afford to ignore

Just What Is... Network Marketing? (£3.50)

This is what the industry has been asking for: a simple, British introduction to network marketing for prospective distributors. Positive in tone but avoiding any hint of 'hype', *Just What Is...* is a prospecting tool that projects the right professional image for your business. Many people also use it as a basic training tool for new distributors.

SIGHT PUBLISHING

The UK's Premier Service To The Network Marketing Industry

Having difficulty finding the training resources and services you need?

We can help you with:

- Our all-new range of leading-edge British books and tapes featuring David Barber, Peter Clothier, Bruce King, Trevor Lowe, Derek Ross and more
- Exclusive distributor for leading US materials
- Bookings for training and motivational seminars, workshops and keynote speeches on: generating momentum; business-building; sponsoring, retailing; teaching; leadership; personal development
- Consultants to corporate teams and leading distributors
- Advice on setting up book distribution services, starter packs, distributor manuals, sales aids and the law relating to network marketing
- Writers and produc ers of recruiting and starter books, tapes and videos for companies and leading distributors.

For more information, just ring us on 01989-564496 or complete the form overleaf.

Yes!

Please send me regular news about books, tapes, events and training services from the Insight Network Marketing Library.

First Name _____ (Mr/Mrs/Miss/Ms)

Last Name _____

Address _____

_____

_____

Postcode _____

Phone _____ AM / PM / Evening

I am especially interested in information on:

• *Prospecting leaflets & booklets*	Yes / No
• *Materials for new distributors*	Yes / No
• *Effective sponsoring & retailing*	Yes / No
• *Self-development*	Yes / No
• *Telephone counselling with David Barber*	Yes / No
• *Bookings with top trainers and speakers*	Yes / No
• *Wholesale price arrangements*	Yes / No

*My MLM company is:*_____

My group size is around _____ *distributors*

*Please **mail** FREE to:*

Insight Publishing
Freepost SWC0330
Ross-on-Wye
HR9 5BR

Or *fax* to 01989-565596

Please also complete the customer feedback form overleaf...

Thank You!

Let us know what you think!

We would greatly appreciate your feedback on:

Any success stories or problems with applying the ideas in the S.T.A.R. Leadership Programme

_____

_____

_____

_____

_____

If you are having success with the S.T.A.R. Programme, please help us spread the message by writing a few words recommending the books to other distributors

_____

_____

_____

_____

_____

_____

Any comments, good or bad, on the service you received from Insight Publishing?

_____

_____

_____

Can we use your comments on our publicity?

Yes ☐   *Yes, with name disguised* ☐   *No* ☐

Please complete the form overleaf and mail FREE to the address provided.